The
DEATH
of
MESSIAH

The
DEATH
of
MESSIAH

Edited by
Kai Kjær-Hansen

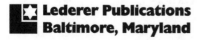

Lederer Publications
Baltimore, Maryland

EDITED BY:
Kai Kjær-Hansen
ASSISTED BY:
Birger Petterson, Bodil F. Skjøtt, David Smith (linguistic editing)

PUBLISHED BY:
Lederer Publications, 6204 Park Heights Avenue, Baltimore, Maryland
21215, 410-358-6471

DISTRIBUTION:
Lederer Distributors, 6204 Park Heights Avenue, Baltimore, Maryland
21215
Caspari Center, P.O.Box 71099, Jerusalem 91710 Israel
Other major book distributors

The Death of Messiah
1. Messiah — Old Testament, New Testament, Qumran, Judaism, Christianity. 2. Messianic Judaism/Jewish Christanity. 3. Lubavitcher/Habad
movement — Menachem Mendel Schneerson. 4. Jewish evangelism/
Missions. I. Kjær-Hansen, Kai, editor.

Printed in the United States of America

ISBN #1-880226-58-8

Contents

Introduction: The Challenge vii

1. Welcome King Messiah 1
    Kai Kjær-Hansen
2. What the Press Wrote about Schneerson 9
    Susan Perlman
3. God's Messiah in the Tanakh 19
    Noam Hendren
4. Qumran, Messiah and Jesus 27
    Ole Andersen
5. The Messiah Who Was Cursed on the Tree 33
    Torleif Elgvin
6. The Messiah Who Died for Our Sins 39
    Sam Nadler
7. The Risen Messiah: Firstfruits of the Resurrection 49
    Barry Rubin
8. Jewish Christianity — The First Century 55
    Arthur F. Glasser
9. The Messianic Idea in Judaism 61
    Louis Goldberg
10. The Habad Movement and Its Messiah 69
    Carol Calise

11. Renewed Interest in Messianic Texts 75
    Tsvi Sadan
12. On Calculating the Time of the Messiah's Appearance ... 83
    Ray Pritz
13. Jewish Objections to Jesus 91
    Arnold Fruchtenbaum
14. What Kind of Person is Jesus? 97
    Walter Riggans
15. The Triune God and the Jew Jesus 101
    Kai Kjær-Hansen
16. The Rebirth of Messianic Judaism 105
    David Sedaca
17. Messianic Believers in Israel and Their Messiah 113
    Bodil F. Skjøtt
18. Jesus, Israels' Messiah — a Messiah for Israel 121
    Tuvya Zaretsky
19. My Way to the Messiah 129
    Stan Telchin
20. The Coming Messiah and the Return of Jesus 135
    Kai Kjær-Hansen

Glossary 139
Selected Bibliography 143
Author Information 147

Introduction:
The Challenge

Jewish theologian Abraham J. Heschel once asked some Christian theologians a challenging question. He asked if the Christian Church had forgotten how the New Testament begins. He then proceeded to quote the first sentence from the first book of the New Testament, the Gospel according to Matthew. In this way he, as a Jew, challenged the Christian Church. For the Church has Jewish roots. If these roots are cut off, the identity of the Christian Church will suffer. Far too often the Church has neglected her Jewish roots.

The evangelist Matthew — with Heschel — still challenges the Christian Church. But really Matthew's challenge begins elsewhere. His challenge is primarily addressed to the Jewish people. His challenge is: A person's identity as a Jew will suffer if the bond to Jesus of Nazareth, the Messiah of the Jews, is severed. He who nevertheless does so will find himself on a collision course with the God of Israel, who has revealed himself in Jesus — or in *Yeshua* as is his name in Hebrew.

The first sentence in Matthew reads as follows: "The book of the genealogy of Jesus the Messiah, the son of David, the son of Abraham."

The signals from Matthew are clear:

Jesus is the Messiah. Jesus of Nazareth is the fulfillment of the promises given by Israel's God to, among others, Abraham, "the first Jew," and David, the great Jewish king.

Jesus is the son of David. Since Jesus is of David's lineage — and he cannot be the Messiah if he is not — then he is relevant to Jews.

Jesus is the son of Abraham. God made a special covenant with Abraham. The Jewish people became God's chosen people. But the election of Abraham even implied good news for non-Jews. Abraham was told: "In you all the families of the earth shall be blessed" (Genesis 12:3). So when Jesus is the son of Abraham, the one who fulfils God's promises, he is relevant to both Jews and non-Jews.

In this book the issue of the Messiah will be treated by a number of people, Jews as well as non-Jews, who have come to faith in Jesus as the Messiah. It is an attempt to reformulate the challenge which Matthew, almost 2000 years ago, presented to the readers of his day.

The question as to who the Messiah is, or was, or might be, or could not have been has been debated down through history by Jews and gentiles.

The point of departure is the renewed interest in this question, not least in Jewish circles. This interest is due to the Habad or Lubavitcher movement. Particularly since the late 1980s part of the movement's followers have claimed that its leader since 1950–1951, Rabbi Menachem Mendel Schneerson, of Brooklyn, New York, was the Messiah. His father-in-law, who was the sixth Lubavitcher rebbe died in 1950; but it took almost a year before Menachem Mendel Schneerson was elected the seventh leader of the movement.

The authors of this book, be they of Jewish or non-Jewish descent, have no calling to be patronizing about the Messianic expectations of the Habad movement. They all share the conviction and belief that Jesus was — and is — Israel's Messiah and agree that Jews as well as non-Jews need Jesus for salvation. Therefore these authors challenge Jews as well as non-Jews.

From different angles, styles and vocabularies, the authors present the issue of the Messiah. Especially for readers not familiar with Jewish vocabulary, Hebrew terminology used in the book is explained in the glossary at the back of the book.

On 12 June 1994 Rabbi Menachem Mendel Schneerson died. Jesus of Nazareth is still alive.

It was with this challenge that the first Jesus-believing Jews met their fellow Jews and the Greco-Roman world almost 2000 years ago.

A similar challenge is presented to people today who want — and dare — to listen to the testimony which the first Jesus-believing Jews gave about their crucified and risen Messiah, Jesus of Nazareth.

He still challenges. He *is* the challenge.

Kai Kjær-Hansen
Jerusalem, 18 June 1994

1

Welcome King Messiah

Kai Kjær-Hansen

Jews do not generally recognize Jesus as the Messiah. Neverthe-less, Jesus is best known and has had the greatest impact among Jewish Messiah figures. Jewish history records several who have claimed to be — or have been regarded as — the Messiah, the most famous being Bar Kokhba, who headed the Great Revolt 132–135AD, and Shabbetai Zevi in the 17th century.

Rabbi Menachem Mendel Schneerson, who died in 1994, will take his place in the long line of Jewish Messiah candidates. His death does not mean that the Habad movement, which he headed from 1950–1951 till his death, will cease regarding him as the Messiah, nor does it mean that they will regard him as a false Messiah. When a Messiah dies, his followers find explana-tions. There are different ways to respond to such explanations, and when dealing with such matters one is inevitably led into the sphere of faith. That is no less true when Jesus-believing Jews and Christians maintain that Jesus was — and is — the Messiah.

Jesus, Bar Kokhba, Shabbetai Zevi and Schneerson

Jesus of Nazareth has for the greater part of Jewish history been considered a *false* Messiah by most Jews. Since the end of the last century some Jewish scholars have tried to give him a place in Jewish history, if not the place of honor, then a place among the really great figures of Jewish history. This does not spring from a belief that he is the Messiah of the Jews, a belief maintained by Messianic Jews, a small yet growing minority of Jews.

Bar Kokhba, called the Son of Star, who was hailed as the Messiah by Rabbi Akiva in 132AD, is often referred to as a *false* Messiah, but there are also other explanations. Bar Kokhba fought in Israel against the Roman occupation army, but his struggle did not bring about redemption as Jews understand it. He was killed by the Romans.

Shabbetai Zevi, who gathered a large following in the 17th century, is now often seen as a *false* Messiah. In 1666, on his journey to the Holy Land, Shabbetai Zevi was imprisoned by the Turkish authorities. He avoided being sentenced to death by converting to Islam. His conversion to Islam did not prevent some of his followers from regarding him as the Messiah. On the contrary, his prophet, Nathan of Gaza, succeeded in exploiting the conversion theologically by saying that for the Messiah to save non-Jews it was necessary that he live in a kind of exile. As late as the outbreak of World War I, there are said to have been 15,000 adherents to this Messianic movement, also called the Dönmeh Sect.

Schneerson's death will affect the Habad sect in as yet unknown ways. But the Habad movement in the years prior to his death in 1994 entertained high expectations that he was the Messiah.

The Habad Movement and Its Messiah

Menachem Mendel Schneerson was born in Russia in 1902. His father, Rabbi Levi Yitzhak Schneerson, was a renowned kabbalist and talmudic scholar. Already by *bar mitzvah* age Menachem Mendel Schneerson was considered a Torah prodigy.

Having studied mathematics and science at the Sorbonne University in Paris he settled in the United States in 1941. At age 48, he assumed leadership of the Habad or Lubavitcher movement — as it is also called after a small town in Byelorussia which became the center of the movement about 1800. At his death in 1994 he was considered "a great man, a towering personality... one of the great, great figures of our days," as stated in *The Jerusalem Post* the day after his death.

The Habad movement, with headquarters in Brooklyn, New York, is active in many parts of the world. According to official information from the movement itself, more than 250,000 children are taught in schools sponsored by the Habad movement. It has more than 3,000 emissaries around the world. The budget is not public, but Jewish sources estimate it to be about $250 million per year. Many of the donations are from Jews who do not themselves adhere to the movement.

It is a fundamental idea in the Habad movement that in every generation there is a potential Messiah. This Messiah is conceived, born, raised and educated in a normal way. There is nothing supernatural about him. There is no need for him to demonstrate supernatural power. The proof that he really *was* the Messiah will come when he rebuilds the Temple in Jerusalem and the Jewish people once again are gathered in the Holy Land to live there peacefully. Again the biblical laws will become the law of the land. The nations will recognize Israel's God and the Jewish people will lead mankind in homage and obedience to God.

The idea of the imminent coming of the Messiah has been central to the Habad movement — right from its early beginning in the first part of the 18th century. Baal Shem Tov, the founder of the movement, describes how in 1746 he experienced the soul's mystical ascent to Paradise. It was then revealed to him that the Messiah would come when the teachings of Baal Shem Tov had been made known all over the world.

It is said about some of the subsequent Hasidic leaders that they tried to hasten the coming of the Messiah through their delight in and observance of the instructions of the law. Many of the leaders were said to go to bed every night expecting the Messiah to come that very night — before they would wake the next day.

In his last years Schneerson urged his followers to hasten the coming of the Messiah through their devotion to Judaism. The underlying idea is that the potential Messiah will reveal himself when there is full return to Judaism.

Very successfully, the Habad movement has spread its message of the imminent coming of the Messiah — particularly since the end of the 1980s.

First Habad followers went out with the slogan: "We want the Messiah now." Although their leader, Schneerson, had not directly declared that he was the Messiah, many of his adherents were nevertheless convinced that he was. The next step was the message on banners, posters and in newspaper advertisements: "Prepare for the coming of the Messiah." Later there were posters and placards with the waving Schneerson accompanied by the text: "Welcome King Messiah." On 29 January 1994 "The World Center for Receiving Moshiach" had inserted a big advertisement in *The Jerusalem Post International* with the clear message: "Rabbi Menachem M. Schneerson is the King Moshiach." While Schneerson, in the spring of 1994, was on a respirator at the Beth Israel Hospital, Manhattan, New York, the Habad movement put advertisements in major American newspapers: "The time of your redemption has come." The advertisement continues: "Rabbi Menachem M. Schneerson Lubavitcher Rebbe King Moshiach." In these advertisements Schneerson is quoted: "Now, do everything you can to bring Moshiach, here and now, immediately."

When a Messiah Dies

Already *before* Schneerson's death there were different views in Habad circles as to how his possible death should be interpreted. His death would not necessarily signify that his adherents would consider him a false Messiah. In the American Jewish magazine *Moment* (April 1993) an expert on the movement, Yosef I. Abramowitz, mentions various possible reactions and explanations by Schneerson's followers.

The explanation as to why the Messianic era did not, after all, come in Schneerson's lifetime will be simple, says Abramowitz. The Jewish people were not worthy to receive the Messiah. Therefore Jews must struggle harder to study the law, particularly the sections that deal with the coming of the Messiah, and must keep on doing good deeds.

A more radical faction within the movement will probably profess that with Schneerson the Messiah *has* come. This will be seen as the first stage in the Messiah drama. The next stage will be the resurrection from the dead and the rebuilding of the Temple, which will take place approximately 40 years later. This explanation will find support in Maimonides, the great medieval Jewish authority. The natural world order will, according to this view, include the death of the Messiah. But this is not the end. They will go on praying for the resurrection of the Messiah (Schneerson) and of all other Jews.

Among Habad followers Schneerson will also be studied after his death. Abramowitz maintains that after Schneerson's death his adherents will still have his picture in their houses and they will continue studying his works. Schneerson's speeches are preserved in large numbers in print and on video. His followers study his words and ascribe the same authoritative importance to them as to the great medieval Jewish authorities, according to Abramowitz.

At Schneerson's death, 12 June 1994, Jewish history scholar Arthur Hertzberg is quoted in *The Jerusalem Post* for saying that the Habad movement will *not* replace Schneerson at all: "There will be no eighth rebbe, not under any circumstances." He points out that this would contradict key Lubavitcher teachings that have always held the messianic age would arrive with the seventh rebbe.

Schneerson was the seventh Lubavitcher rebbe.

Only the future can tell how Schneerson's death will influence the movement. No matter how his death is explained, some of his followers must be greatly disappointed, as followers of Jesus were in the days after his death.

But We Had Hoped

Frustration, disappointment and a defeatist attitude marked the disciples of Jesus after his death. In the Gospels there are several instances which show that they had expected him to establish the kingdom for Israel immediately. When he talked about his death, indeed the necessity of his death, his disciples rebuked him; it did not match their expectations. Therefore he had to rebuke them severely. It was necessary that he suffer and die, he explained. Without his vicarious, redemptive death, no salvation was possible.

The situation in which the disciples' frustrated messianic expectations find their strongest expression is perhaps the scene in which two of his disciples are on their way to Emmaus. The risen Jesus meets them but they do not recognize him. The account in Luke 24:13–27 is worth recalling:

> [13]That very day two of them were going to a village named Emmaus, about seven miles from Jerusalem, [14]and talking with each other about all these things that had happened. [15]While they were talking and discussing together, Jesus himself drew near and went with them. [16]But their eyes were kept from recognizing him. [17]And he said to them, "What is this conversation which you are holding with each other as you walk?" And they stood still, looking sad. [18]Then one of them, named Cleopas, answered him, "Are you the only visitor to Jerusalem who does not know the things that have happened there in these days?" [19]And he said to them, "What things?" And they said to him, "Concerning Jesus of Nazareth, who was a prophet mighty in deed and word before God and all the people, [20]and how our chief priests and rulers delivered him up to be condemned to death, and crucified him. [21]But we had hoped that he was the one to redeem Israel. Yes, and besides all this, it is now the third day since this happened. [22]Moreover, some women of our company amazed us. They were at the tomb early in the

morning and did not find his body; [23]and they came back saying that they had even seen a vision of angels, who said that he was alive. [24]Some of those who were with us went to the tomb, and found it just as the women had said; but him they did not see."

[25]And he said to them, "O foolish men, and slow of heart to believe all that the prophets have spoken! [26]Was it not necessary that the Christ should suffer these things and enter into his glory?" [27]And beginning with Moses and all the prophets, he interpreted to them in all the scriptures the things concerning himself.

Before and After

Readers of *The Jerusalem Post*, the English daily newspaper in Israel, are every day reminded of facts which have influenced our history decisively. There are three dates. First the Christian date, 1994; then the Jewish date from the creation of the world, 5754; and at last the Muslim date, 1414 (lunar years) after Mohammed's *hejira* (emigration) to Medina in 622.

A Jew may not like this, nor for that matter a nominal Christian — but it is a fact that the greater part of the world's population relates their lives to Jesus of Nazareth. This is also the case when it is disguised behind a BCE (Before Common Era) instead of BC (Before Christ [Messiah]) or CE (Common Era) instead of AD (Anno Domini = year of the Lord).

In the day of Bar Kokhba there were also attempts at a new calendar. Archaeologists have found silver coins, stamped in Israel under Bar Kokhba, with the inscription: "Year Two of the Freedom of Israel."

This freedom under Bar Kokhba did not last long. The practice, which could be observed on notice boards in some restaurants in the early 1990s in Jerusalem, of cutting the picture of President Washington out of an American one-dollar bill replacing it with a picture of Schneerson will probably not last long either. Few can imagine that *The Jerusalem Post* will introduce a fourth date, year 1 after Schneerson.

As a believer in Jesus, there is every reason to go on dating one's life from Jesus the Messiah and to go on saying to the living Messiah: "Welcome King Messiah!"

2

What the Press Wrote About Schneerson

Susan Perlman

Menachem Mendel Schneerson became Grand Rabbi, or Rebbe, of the Lubavitcher Movement in 1951. The quantity of written material by him and on him in the past 43 years has been monumental. However, only in recent years did the press focus on the messianic emphasis in his writings and speeches:

> As the Rebbe sees it, the whole world, not just the Jewish people, is today a sinking vessel. According to the Scriptures, turmoil and catastrophe will precede the coming of the Messiah.... More than any of his predecessors, Rebbe Schneerson dwells on the messianic theme (*New York Magazine*, 28 June 1982).

The reporter Dorit Phyllis Gary went on to say that while

the Rebbe never actually declared himself to be the Messiah, he did not contradict his followers who likened him to the prophet Moses. She also pointed out that in Jewish tradition it is held that there is a potential Messiah in every generation and that Schneerson has said,

> ... in every generation there is one who so towers over his contemporaries ... that he is the head of his generation.... In the past generation that person was the previous Lubavitcher Rebbe.

She concluded with the statement, "Clearly, he believes that in this generation that person is himself." This speculation continued for almost a decade.

Lubavitcher administrator, Yossi Raichik, says, "Every generation has a candidate. And in this generation he's [Schneerson's] definitely the best one" (*The Wall Street Journal*, 7 September 1990). Top aide, Rabbi Krinsky says, "I don't know of anyone around now more suitable to fill the shoes of the Messiah than the Rebbe" (*The Wall Street Journal*, 21 December 1989).

The Eschatological Implications of the Gulf War

The speculation culminated in the Persian Gulf Crisis of 1991. It was then that Schneerson announced what he saw as eschatological implications to the Gulf War. Headlines in *The Jerusalem Post* and on the *Jewish Telegraphic Agency* wire read, "Rebbe says Gulf crisis foretells arrival of messiah."

> Schneerson said the Midrash tells of a great agitation that will involve many nations and culminate in an earth shaking confrontation in the Persian Gulf.... [The cataclysm will] herald the coming of the Messiah, who will stand on the roof of the Temple and announce to Israel, "The time of your redemption is come" (*Jewish Telegraphic Agency*, August 1991).

The *Jewish Chronicle* of London (30 November 1991) intimated the messianic ramifications of the events as well:

> For over 1900 years the Jews have shouted "ad mosai?" ("until when?"). The previous Rebbe declared that all that was needed to prepare for the Moshiach's coming was to "polish the buttons." That preparation has now been completed.

Yet at that point in time, most of his followers were still cautious in forthrightly pronouncing him Messiah. Nevertheless, they put out full page advertisements citing the Gulf War victory, the exodus of Soviet Jews, Israel's safety amidst the Scud missiles, and the fall of Communism as a prelude to the final redemption.

Rabbi Schneerson — The Messiah or Not?

In response to a question as to whether the Rebbe himself was being regarded as Messiah, Menahem Brod, Israeli spokesman for Habad, commented that "such expressions had come from only a few individuals, though the Rebbe had forbidden his followers to make such statements." The *Northern California Jewish Bulletin* (31 May 1991) recorded the following exchange between Rabbi Manis Friedman, a Habad lecturer, and a colleague. Friedman said:

> "I can't think of a more likely candidate." Rabbi Yosef Langer rejoined with, "You're not supposed to speculate. It would be nice if my Rebbe was the moshiach, but I'll go with the flow."

Another disciple, Rabbi Chayim Bergstein of Congregation Bais Chabad in Michigan noted that it is undebatable that the Messiah would be a descendant of David and that Schneerson is a descendant of the House of David:

> I'm not saying he is or isn't Mashiach, but there is no one

as learned, as pious, as caring, as courageous, as intellectual and as influential in this generation. These are all the traits Maimonides identified as belonging to Mashiach (Detroit Jewish News, 3 January 1992).

According to *Jewish Telegraphic Agency* reporter Debra Nussbaum Cohen, when Kfar Habad, a Lubavitcher community in Israel, wanted to expand their settlement in 1992, representatives came to Schneerson for a blessing and asked him to reveal that he is the Messiah. He did not respond. However, his followers interpreted his decision to allow the building of a house for him at Kfar Habad (given that he had never set foot in Israel) as an omen that he would reveal his identity to be that of Messiah.

Certainly many of his followers at this point were making it known that they believed he was indeed the Messiah.

"Rabbi Schneerson is the Messiah. I don't even have to think twice about it," said a 45-year-old woman who was shopping near Kfar Chabad's grocery store and gave her name only as Rachel. "We talk about it a lot and we are waiting for the big event" (*Associated Press,* 5 March 1992).

Schneerson suffered a stroke in early March 1992, but this did not deter his faithful followers. Yossi Schneerson from Kiryat Malachi responded:

I feel he is the man. Moses also had physical problems, he could not speak properly. The Rebbe is only flesh and blood. His soul is that of the Messiah (*The Jerusalem Post,* International Edition, 14 March 1992).

Habad's active campaigning to crown Schneerson Messiah has included over 200 billboards in Israel, full-page advertisements with titles like "Moshiach is coming and we must make the final preparations," and bumper stickers.

A False Messiah

One of the most interesting commentaries on this messianic fervor was entitled "Expecting the Messiah: An ultra-Orthodox sect says the Redeemer is due to arrive any day now — and he might be an American," by Lisa Beyer. She reported for *Time Magazine* (23 March 1992) on some of the opposition to Schneerson as a candidate for Messiah:

> Eliezer Schach, one of Israel's leading ultra-Orthodox rabbis, has publicly called Schneerson "insane," an "infidel" and "a false Messiah."

Another opponent, Knesset member Avraham Ravitz, said:

> It's crazy to force the Messiah to come by selling him like Coca Cola, with jingles and stickers and billboards (*Time Magazine,* 23 March 1992).

Other critics voiced concern that the group (Lubavitcher Hasidim) may be creating the conditions for large-scale spiritual disillusionment:

> "If you convince people that the Messiah is coming and he doesn't," says Amnon Levy, author of a book on the ultra-Orthodox, "a whole generation may lose its faith" (*Time Magazine,* 23 March 1992).

Schneerson's 90th birthday became a media event in April 1992. Among the honors was a celebration in Washington, D.C. with Nobel Laureate Elie Wiesel bringing the tribute and many United States congressmen in attendance. May 1992 produced a "Moshiach Parade" down Fifth Avenue in Manhattan with tens of thousands cheering. The parade was organized by the "International Campaign to Help Bring Moshiach." More full-page advertisements and additional critics such as Rabbi Morris Rubinstein made their sentiments known:

I urge the Habad Messianism to be categorically rejected. Every Messianic Movement in the past brought nothing but disappointment and grief. This movement has the potential for a spiritual Jonestown disaster with many apostasizing as in the past. Every personal Messiah has sooner or later taken on the persona of divinity — Jesus of Nazareth, Sabbetai Zevi and Jacob Frank. It can very easily happen again.... Habad is not an insignificant movement in Judaism — but the time has nevertheless come to call its bluff; to openly and unequivocally reject its messianic pretensions (*National Jewish Post and Opinion,* 23 September 1992).

What Happens If the Messiah Dies?

January of 1993 marked the start of the Rebbe's 43rd year as Grand Rabbi of Lubavitch. Many followers anticipated he would use the occasion to announce his Messiahship. Video cameras beamed their pictures to Lubavitcher centers world-wide. Seven thousand chanted the words, "Long live our master, our teacher and our rabbi, the King Messiah, live forever!" and Schneerson nodded his head to the rhythm of the chant but did not accept the "crown." This increased enthusiasm to proclaim him Messiah split the more moderate Lubavitcher Hasidim from the radical Messianists. What made the debate most disconcerting was the fact that Schneerson's physical condition prevented him from speaking. All his non-verbal action, therefore, was subject to interpretation. Some followers would take a nod to mean he was agreeing that he was indeed the Messiah. Others would interpret the same gesture differently.

A comprehensive article funded by a grant to the Religious News Service was published in the April 1993 issue of the Jewish magazine, *Moment,* entitled "What Happens If the Rebbe Dies?" Its author, Yosef I. Abramowitz, dealt with (among other things) the two factions of Lubavitchers and who would prevail upon the Rebbe's death:

Chassidic burial sites become holy places for their followers and will, in the case of Lubavitch, determine if the power center will be in Crown Heights with the mainstreamers or in Israel with the radicals.... The former Rebbe and his wife, as well as Menachem Mendel's wife are buried in Queens.... On the southern tip of the Mount of Olives, overlooking the Golden Gate on the eastern wall of the Temple mount, through which tradition says the moshiach will enter Jerusalem, the Lubavitch cemetery is undergoing some light reconstruction. If the Rebbe's body is brought to Jerusalem, it will be a signal that the control of the movement has passed to the radical messianists in Israel.

Reports in May of 1993 indicated that the Rebbe's health took a turn for the better. Rabbi Yehuda Krinsky reported that "the Rebbe is not only responding to questions, but can initiate conversations. He has also regained much motion in his right side, although the left remains paralyzed" (*South African Herald Times*, 21 May 1993). However, there was a void on news on him for a period of months. In November 1993 it was reported that he was brought to a hospital for tests. On 31 December 1993 a *Jewish Telegraphic Agency* release explained:

The Lubavitcher Rebbe's health has deteriorated to the point where he is almost completely blinded by cataracts, has lost physical mobility and is a virtual prisoner in his own room, say medical experts who have been involved in his care as consultants.

The advertisements concerning him as Messiah began not long after. In large type the ads proclaimed "The Lubavitcher Rebbe Rabbi Menachem M. Schneerson is the King Moshiach. Now is the time to accept his kingship!" (*The Jerusalem Post*, International Edition, 29 January 1994). There was a Bat Yam address at the bottom of the ad.

Then Schneerson's health deteriorated further as he suffered another stroke. Pamela Druckerman of the *Jewish Telegraphic Agency* (15 March 1994) reported:

> As Lubavitch Rebbe Menachem Mendel Schneerson lies unconscious in a Manhattan intensive care unit following a stroke last week, some Lubavitch leaders are viewing his illness, along with the recent shooting of Chasidic students on the Brooklyn Bridge as a sign that redemption is near.

Ms. Druckerman continued,

> ...Neil Gillman, an associate professor of philosophy at the Jewish Theological Seminary in New York and long-time observer of the Lubavitch movement, predicted the Rebbe's death could not be justified along the same theological lines that propelled him into potential Messiah status, without rupturing the movement. "They will quickly conclude that the generation wasn't ready, that they weren't good enough," Gillman said, referring to the Jewish belief that there is a potential messiah in every generation who will be revealed if and when the world is ready. "But for the Lubavitchers — who have invested tremendously in a version of history that many say points to Schneerson as the Messiah — there is a determination to hold onto that vision."

Dead and Buried...

On Sunday, 12 June 1994, Menachem Mendel Schneerson died at Beth Israel Medical Center in New York. In Israel, some of his followers denied the reports of his death saying, "He's the Messiah. He's not dead." *The New York Times* reported (13 June 1994) that thousands of his disciples came to the Crown Heights headquarters "to mourn a teacher and scholar that most of them had hoped would reveal himself to be the Messiah before he died."

Others flew to New York with the hope that "they could be present when Rabbi Schneerson would somehow proclaim his kingship before being buried."

Schneerson was buried next to his father-in-law, the previous Grand Rabbi, in the Old Montefiore Cemetery in Queens, New York — not at the Mount of Olives as others had speculated.

Yet his followers have not given up on a messianic hope. Rabbi Sholom Weinberg, who made a pilgrimage to the cemetery where Schneerson is buried, postulated that this could well be a test of faith, for though he would have preferred to see Schneerson proclaim himself the Messiah, Weinberg still believed that a Messiah would come:

> The fact that the Rebbe obviously passed away and is not in a position to be the redeemer has nothing to do with the concept of the redeemer himself (*The New York Times,* 14 June 1994).

3

God's Messiah in the Tanakh

Noam Hendren

Is there a "Messiah" in the House?

"Messiah," as a technical term for the promised Davidic ruler-redeemer, occurs rarely, if at all, in the entire Tanakh (i.e. the Jewish Scriptures, the first part of the Bible). The most likely candidates for a technical use of the term are found in Psalms 2 and 89 and, especially, in the (relatively) late book of Daniel (9:25–26). While "the Messiah" may not appear in the Tanakh under this specific title, the choice of this term (during the Second Temple Period) to encapsulate the biblical messianic hope is, nevertheless, quite appropriate.

In biblical usage, the Hebrew term *mashiach* designates "one anointed (with oil and/or with the Holy Spirit) and thereby set apart and equipped to perform a special task for God." By anointing with oil, the high priest was consecrated for service in the Tabernacle (Exodus 29:1–9; cf. Leviticus 4:3, etc., "the anointed priest"). Similarly, the prophet Elisha was to be anointed as Elijah's successor (1 Kings. 19:16). In one place, even a pagan king (Cyrus) is referred to, metaphorically, as God's anointed one, because he had been selected and enabled by God to fulfill a specific task: the restoration of Israel from captivity (Isaiah 45:1).

But it is particularly in the anointing of the kings of Israel that *mashiach* gained its messianic connotations. "The anointed of the Lord" appears as a designation for the king of Israel throughout the Scripture (e.g. 1 Samuel 2:10; 24:6; Psalms 18:50; Lamentations 4:20). In David's own anointing at the hands of Samuel (1 Samuel 16:13) the ramifications of this title are more fully seen. As Samuel poured out the oil upon David as a symbol of his selection and consecration to be the next king of Israel, God himself "anointed" David with his Spirit, empowering him to fulfill his divine calling.

Messianic Roots

The Messianic hope is rooted in the corruption of mankind and all creation following the rebellion in Eden. The immediate effects of mankind's sin: the awareness of true moral guilt, alienation from a holy God, and the breakdown of human relationships in the selfish attempt to "save one's own skin," were quickly followed by God's direct curse both on man himself and on the world which had been placed under his care and responsibility (Genesis 3:7–19; cf. 1:26–28; 2:15). In sad contrast to the divine blessing which attended man's creation and installment as God's regent over all the earth, now sin, suffering, and eventual death became the lot of every man, and the creation shared the fate of her master (Genesis 4–5; cf. Romans 8:20–21).

In this context of curse and corruption which man's sin engendered, the first hint of messianic redemption was given by God himself. Addressing the serpent, the Lord promised,

> I will put enmity between you and the woman, and between your seed and her seed; he shall bruise you on the head, and you shall bruise him on the heel (Genesis 3:15).

The promise that one day a descendent of the woman, who was the first victim and tool of Satan, would deal a fatal blow to the ultimate source of the sin and suffering which had befallen mankind, gave hope that one day the effects of sin would be reversed and sin itself would be eliminated.

Messiah, the Son of David

The hope of the ultimate redemption of man and the world and their restoration to their original blessed state was reiterated in the promise which God made to Abraham that "in you all the families of the earth would be blessed" (Genesis 12:3). The redeemer would be descended not only from the woman (Genesis 3:15) but from Abraham (cf. Genesis 22:18, "In your seed all the nations of the earth will be blessed"). The results of that redemption were described in Jacob's prophecy that a descendant of Judah would be the one to rule among his people and all peoples, bringing a state of Edenic blessing to the world (Genesis 49:10–12).

The messianic idea in its fullest sense begins with the covenant which God made with David early in his reign as king. This covenant is recorded twice in Scripture (in 2 Samuel 7 and the later version in 1 Chronicles 17) and it provides the biblical framework for the messianic hope and the foundation for the messianic predictions given by the prophets of Israel. The intimate connection between the hoped-for redeemer and the house of David, based on this covenant, is reflected in the common designation, "Messiah, the son of David."

The Davidic covenant was made after God had established David as King over all Israel, eliminated his rivals from Saul's house, defeated Israel's key enemies, the Philistines, and aided David in capturing Jerusalem and setting up his capital there (2 Samuel 1–6). David, in turn, wanted to build a "house" (Temple) for the Lord in Jerusalem (2 Samuel 7:1–4). In refusing David's request, God made an unconditional promise to raise up a line of descendants from the house of David who would forever rule as the sole legitimate kings of Israel (2 Samuel 7:5–16).

The covenant promises a perpetual "seed" to David. "Seed"

is a collective term which can refer either to the entire line of David's descendants viewed as a group or to any single individual in the line, depending on the context. In 2 Samuel, while the whole line is in view, special emphasis is given to Solomon ("who will come forth from your bowels," 7:12), whose right to rule was most likely to be challenged by lingering pro-Saul sentiment. Solomon would build the Temple which David had proposed and God would see that Solomon's own kingdom and his dynasty's right to rule ("throne") would endure, although he would correct the king like a father corrects his son (7:13–15). This promise was a special comfort to David, whose predecessor Saul had been unable to perpetuate his rule in his sons (vv. 16–19).

By the time 1 Chronicles was written, the Babylonian captivity had caused a break in the Davidic dynasty which had never been mended. No longer did anyone question the legitimacy of the Davidic right to rule, but the nation yearned for the appearance of that Davidic ruler-redeemer whom the prophets had predicted (cf. Psalms 89:19–52). In his version of the covenant, the Chronicler focuses on this greatest son of David ("who shall be of your sons," 17:11), who will rebuild the Temple of the Lord (v. 12) and to whom God will be a father without the need for correction (v. 13). This son of David is the ultimate fulfillment of the covenant who will not only rule on David's throne, but will function both as God's high priest ("I will settle him in My house [Temple]") and as regent in God's kingdom ("in My kingdom") forever (v. 14).

Messiah the King

The presentation of the Davidic King-Priest in Chronicles encapsulates the prophetic revelation concerning the Messiah given between 950–450BC. The various prophetic passages tend to focus either on Messiah in his function as conquering King who establishes God's kingdom on earth or as the Priest-servant who brings spiritual redemption by providing in himself the perfect atonement for sin.

Isaiah 11:1–10 is perhaps the best known messianic passage

in the Scriptures. Here Isaiah focuses on the nature and activities of the Messiah in establishing God's Kingdom on earth, restoring the creation to its original pristine state.

The passage opens by presenting the physical descent of the redeemer and his spiritual anointing for service (11:1–2): "Then a shoot will spring from the stem of Jesse, and a branch from his roots will bear fruit. And the Spirit of the Lord will rest on Him..." The redeemer would be a descendent ("shoot," "branch") of Jesse, David's father, and would be anointed by God's Spirit as David himself was. He is therefore God's Messiah (anointed One). The seven characteristics of the anointing Spirit (see v. 2) will enable the Messiah to establish justice, righteousness and peace on the earth (vv. 3–5). As a result, all creation will be restored to Edenic conditions, and all men will know (be in right relationship with) the Lord (vv. 6–10).

Isaiah 9:6–7 (vv. 5–6 in Hebrew Bibles) adds crucial detail concerning the Messiah's person and rule:

> For a child will be born to us, a son will be given to us;
> And the government will rest on His shoulders; And His
> name will be called Wonderful Counselor, Mighty God,
> Eternal Father, Prince of Peace.

He is a man, a "child...born" to rule. But he is also more than a man, as his names clearly indicate. The name "Mighty God" in particular appears only twice in this precise form (in Hebrew) in the Scriptures, here and in Isaiah 10:21. There the term is a clear designation for "YHVH, the Holy One of Israel" (cf. 10:20).

As the "Mighty God" and "Father of Eternity," the Messiah is able to rule "on the throne of David and over his kingdom... forevermore" (9:7), thus guaranteeing the ultimate fulfillment of God's promise to David.

Isaiah's contemporary, Micah, adds to our picture by indicating the birthplace of Messiah who will "shepherd His flock in the strength of the Lord" and who "will be our peace" (5:2–5; in

Hebrew Bibles vv. 1–4). The "ruler" would be born in Bethlehem of Judah, the birthplace of his father David. This connection emphasizes the unique relationship between David who received the promise of God and the Messiah who fulfills the covenant, as type and antitype. [An "antitype" does not oppose its "type"; rather, it "fills the shoes" of its type, even surpassing it in some ways.] It is not surprising that several passages simply refer to Messiah by the name "David" (Jeremiah 30:9; Ezekiel 34:23f; 37:24f.; Hosea 3:5).

Messiah the King-Priest

The uniqueness of the Messiah is especially evident in his dual function as king and priest. Normally, due to the restriction of the priesthood to the tribe of Levi and the kingship to the tribe of Judah, no one individual could hold both offices. But the Messiah's mission extended beyond a physical restoration of man and the world to Edenic perfection. He was also to bring a spiritual restoration of sinful man to God by providing full atonement for sin — hence his priestly function.

The Davidic Messiah is designated as King-Priest in Zechariah 6:9–13 (cf. also Psalm 110). There the high priest Joshua ben Jehozadak is "crowned" as a type of the Messiah to come. God instructs Zechariah to interpret the action as referring to Messiah, called here "Branch" (the Messianic title based on Isaiah 4:2; 11:1; and Jeremiah 23:5–6). This one "will build the temple of the Lord…" and he will "sit and rule on His throne. Thus, He will be a priest on his throne…." As the King-Priest, Messiah will be enthroned in God's house — which he himself will build — forever (1 Chronicles 17:12, 14; cf. Ezekiel 43:7).

The Ministry of Messiah as Priest

Messiah's ministry as priest is particularly detailed in the suffering Servant passages of Isaiah (chapters 42, 49, 50, 53). Isaiah 49:1–6 reveals the goal and objectives of the Messianic Priest's ministry, while Isaiah 52:13–53:12 give us the means and course of his work.

Isaiah 52:13–53:12 (which is discussed more fully elsewhere

in this book) focuses on the atoning sacrifice which Messiah the Priest-Servant would provide. The Servant, who would one day be greatly exalted, must first be hideously disfigured and humiliated in order to "sprinkle many nations" and thus cleanse them from their sins (52:13–15; cf. usage of "sprinkle" in Leviticus 4:6). The course of these shocking developments is described in chapter 53.

Rather than being accepted and revered, Isaiah reveals that when Messiah would appear, he would be rejected — even despised and considered accursed of God — by his own people (vv. 1–3). His suffering would be as great as it was unjust, seeing that he would be innocent of any wrongdoing and totally undeserving of his horrible death (vv. 7–9). But his suffering would not be without purpose, for as the only truly and totally innocent sufferer, he would offer himself as a perfect and final sacrifice for sin (vv. 4–6, 10–12). Having fulfilled his priestly and sacrificial ministry perfectly and willingly, the Servant Messiah would be restored to life that he might enjoy the fruits of his labor and the glory which is his just reward (vv. 10, 12).

Messiah and the Coming of Redemption

But when will this Messiah come? In the "last days," following the chastisement of her dispersion, Israel as a nation will repent, seeking a right relationship with God and the coming of Messiah, son of David (cf. Deuteronomy 4:29–30). But has Israel not sought the coming of Messiah in every generation? Isaiah 10:21 declares that "the remnant of Jacob" will return "to El Gibbor," Messiah the Mighty God of Isaiah 9:6. In other words, Israel must not just seek "a Messiah" but "the Messiah" whom God sends both as Priest-Servant and King. Only then "the Redeemer will come to Zion, and to those who turn from transgression in Jacob" (Isaiah 59:20).

By God's direct intervention, Israel will suddenly realize that Yeshua El Gibbor, who was "pierced," died and was raised from the dead before the Second Temple's destruction, is their only Messiah. They will look unto him for salvation, as Israel in the wilderness looked unto the bronze snake (Numbers 21:8–9), and they will be redeemed.

4

Qumran, Messiah and Jesus

Ole Andersen

"Israel was not exiled before twenty-four groups of heretics had arisen." This description of Second Temple Judaism, just before the destruction of the Temple in 70AD, is ascribed to Rabbi Johanan of the third century in The Jerusalem Talmud, *Sanhedrin* 10:6. One should not attach too much importance to the exact figure of 24, but there is no doubt that the overall picture of Second Temple Judaism given by Rabbi Johanan is correct. The last centuries of the Second Temple Period saw the appearance of a number of different sects, spiritual movements and religious groups within Judaism.

Some of the groups are well-known from the rabbinic literature, from the Jewish historian Josephus, and from the New Testament and other sources. This is true of the Pharisees, the Sadducees, the Essenes and some of the national-religious groups leading the revolt against the Roman occupation. The relationship between the groups was rather complicated. The Pharisees and the Sadducees agreed on some issues against the Essenes, but in other respects the Essenes and the Pharisees shared a common view against the Sadducees, and so on. The actual number of members of the different groups was relatively small, but the Pharisees had an especially strong influence on the thinking and living of many Jews of Israel.

The finding of the Dead Sea Scrolls has thrown new and astonishing light on the complicated phenomenon of sects and groups of Second Temple Judaism. Suddenly scholars got access to Second Temple Period writings reflecting the way of life and the faith of one of these groups. Since 1990 a renewed interest in the Dead Sea Scrolls has arisen simultaneously with extensive changes in the project of publication of the many thousands of scroll-fragments. Particularly the relationship between the group behind the scrolls and the first congregation of Jewish believers in Jesus has been the subject of an intense discussion. Two popular books on this relationship have been sold in very large numbers in many countries. One of them claims that the main characters of the scrolls are Jesus himself and John the Baptist, while the other book argues that they are James, Jesus' brother, and the apostle Paul.

Before taking a closer look at these sensational claims we shall briefly outline some of the facts of the Dead Sea Scrolls and the group which composed them.

The Dead Sea Scrolls of Qumran

The Dead Sea Scrolls were found during the years 1947 to 1956 in 11 caves near Qumran on the northwest shore of the Dead Sea. Altogether remains of about 800 scrolls were found. A few of them were fairly intact, but most had only survived as small fragments.

The library in the caves included copies of the books of the Hebrew Bible and other ancient Jewish writings. Some of the scrolls clearly reflected the life and faith of a particular Jewish group of the Second Temple Period. Today the vast majority of scholars agree that the members of this group were the owners of the library in the caves, that they lived in the nearby settlement of Qumran, and that they were more or less closely associated with the Essenes living all over Israel.

The Qumran community was convinced that Israel at large was living in sin and error. All the different groups of the Jewish people had forsaken the true worship of the God of Israel and the true understanding of the Torah of Moses. That had been the situation through all the generations since Babylonian King Nebuchadnezzar ruined Jerusalem and the Temple in 586BC. But now God had demonstrated his faithfulness towards Israel by causing a small group of Jews to repent. After 20 years of searching for the truth, this group got a strong and charismatic leader in a person called the "Teacher of Righteousness." The scrolls do not give much help in identifying the teacher, but two things are stated clearly: he was a priest, and his teaching and interpretation of the Bible determined the outlook and beliefs of the group.

Some members of the group refused to accept the teacher and parted from him and his followers. The leader of this breakaway group is called the "Liar" in the scrolls. Another opponent of the teacher and his congregation was the "Wicked Priest" who was in power in Jerusalem. At some time in the second or first century BC, the congregation left Jerusalem and established its center and library at Qumran near the Dead Sea.

The community's belief that all other Jews were in error, together with its constant conflicts with other Jewish groups, led it to a severe and harsh condemnation of everybody else. They alone possessed the truth. They alone were the remnant of Israel, elected by God in a situation of general ungodliness in Israel.

The members of the community were sure that they were living in the last generation. The emergence of the community ushered in the eschatological era when God would overthrow the rule of the godless and establish his kingdom. The community itself would play an important role in the events of the last days. But they also looked forward to the coming of two messianic figures: a priestly Messiah (the "Messiah of Aaron") and a lay Davidic Messiah (the "Messiah of Israel"). The exact roles of the

Messiahs are not clearly described in the scrolls, but their appearances would result in the final and everlasting bliss.

Sensational Identifications

On the basis of the dating of the scrolls, their contents and the archaeology of Qumran, most scholars date the beginning of the community to the mid-second century BC. According to this view the "Wicked Priest" is either the Hasmonean high priest and ruler Jonathan (161–142BC) or his brother and successor Simon (142–135BC). The "Teacher of Righteousness" is a pious Jewish leader who refused to recognize the religious and political leadership in Jerusalem, and the "Liar" is the leader of another (probably Pharisaic) religious group.

In recent years two widely circulated popular books have advanced differing theories. The first theory is put forward by Michael Baigent and Richard Leigh in *The Dead Sea Scrolls Deception* (London 1991). Baigent and Leigh are heavily dependent on professor Robert Eisenman, California State University. According to Baigent and Leigh the Dead Sea Scrolls deal with persons and events known from the New Testament. The "Teacher of Righteousness" is a code name for James, Jesus' brother. The New Testament tells that James was the leader of the first congregation of Jewish believers in Jesus in Jerusalem. But according to Baigent and Leigh this congregation was in reality a very militant and zealous Jewish sect which, under the leadership of James, was in the forefront of the Jewish revolt against Rome (66–70AD). The community in Qumran belonged to the same movement. The main adversary of James and his sect was the Jewish pro-Roman high priest Ananias (c. 47–59AD) who is the "Wicked Priest" of the scrolls. In the beginning Paul, too, fought against the rebels, but later he joined the movement. He was not really accepted, however, and after a dispute with the leaders he was exiled from Israel. While abroad he fabricated the stories about Jesus' miracles, the virgin-birth, the resurrection, etc. The leaders of the movement back in Israel of course rejected Paul's forgeries and named him, in the scrolls, the "Liar."

In the book *Jesus & the Riddle of the Dead Sea Scrolls: Unlocking the Secrets of His Life Story* (San Francisco 1992) the Australian theologian Barbara Thiering proposes an even more sensational theory. According to Thiering the "Teacher of Righteousness" is John the Baptist, the New Testament forerunner of Jesus. The "Wicked Priest" and the "Liar" are two different code names of one person, namely Jesus. On the basis of these identifications, Thiering composes an imaginative story of the "real" Jesus who survived the crucifixion, was married twice, had several children and died in Rome much later.

In spite of their mutual exclusiveness, the theories of Thiering and of Baigent and Leigh share several serious problems. First, their theories are in blatant disagreement with the scholarly consensus on the dating of the Dead Sea Scrolls. Scholars date the scrolls on the basis of archaeological evidence, historical references in the scrolls, the form of the handwriting (paleography), and carbon-14 tests. The oldest Dead Sea Scroll mentioning the "Teacher of Righteousness" is dated to 75–50BC, and this scroll is a copy of the text, not the original (the scholarly designation of the scroll is 4QD^b). This means that the copy is 100 years or more older than the original could have been, had the "Teacher of Righteousness" been John the Baptist or James. Even if allowance is made for some possible inaccuracy of the dating, this renders the theories of Thiering and Baigent and Leigh impossible.

Another serious problem with the theories is their incompatibility with the scrolls themselves. One example is the description in one of the scrolls (4QpHab VIII) of the "Wicked Priest" as a ruler of Israel who was corrupted by wealth and power. Even though nobody will claim that Jesus ever was the ruler of Israel, Thiering still insists that the "Wicked Priest" is a code name for Jesus. Moreover, the theories totally contradict the picture given by other historical sources, e.g. Josephus and the New Testament, of the different religious groups at the end of the Second Temple Period.

As a consequence of these and other problems, practically all scholars, including Jews, Catholics, Evangelicals and non-affiliated, have rejected the theories of Thiering and Baigent and Leigh as unfounded and impossible.

More Light on Ancient Judaism

Jesus, John the Baptist, James and Paul are not mentioned in the Dead Sea Scrolls. But that is not appalling, for neither are Hillel, Shammai, Herod the Great, or King Agrippa mentioned!

Nevertheless the Dead Sea Scrolls are important to the understanding of the New Testament, because they throw more light on the ancient Judaism to which Jesus and his followers belonged. Today it is clearer than ever that the Jewish people of the first century AD were divided into many different religious movements and groups. Rabbi Johanan was right! At the end of the Second Temple period there was one Jewish people, but many religious groups. One of these groups within the Jewish people was the Qumran community; another was the movement of "Messianic Jews" — Jews who believed that Jesus from Nazareth fulfilled the prophecies of the Hebrew Bible and therefore was the Messiah of Israel.

5

The Messiah Who Was Cursed on the Tree

Torleif Elgvin

A crucified Messiah is an impossibility — the one hanged on the tree is a traitor or a blasphemer. Hanging on the cross he is accursed by God and men. Such was the priestly doctrine in the days of Jesus, as some texts from the Dead Sea Scrolls have revealed.

In Deuteronomy 21:22–23 we find the following law:

> If a man guilty of a capital offense is put to death and his body is hung on a tree, you must not leave his body on the tree overnight. Be sure to bury him that same day, because anyone who is hung on a tree is accursed by God. You must not defile the land the Lord your God is giving you as an inheritance.

A Radical Reinterpretation

In the second century BC an author close to the Essene community made a new edition of the laws of Deuteronomy, incorporating verses from Leviticus and Numbers as well as priestly teaching from his own time. He published this new edition as authoritative Torah of God. In this book, the *Temple Scroll*, we meet a radical reinterpretation of these verses from Deuteronomy:

> If a man informs against his people and delivers his people up to a foreign nation, and does harm to his people, you shall hang him on the tree so that he dies. On the word of two and three witnesses shall he be put to death, and they shall hang him on the tree. If a man has committed a crime punishable by death, because he has defected into the midst of the nations and has cursed his people, the children of Israel, you shall hang him also on the tree so that he dies. And their bodies shall not remain upon the tree, but you shall bury them the same day, for those who hang on the tree are accursed by God and men, you must not defile the land which I give you as an inheritance (*Temple Scroll* 64:6–13).

In Deuteronomy it is not clear whether the evildoer should be hanged alive upon the tree or only the corpse after he is executed. The *Temple Scroll* clearly ordains that certain evildoers shall be executed by being hanged alive on the tree. The word *tree* can mean a tree, a pole or a cross. "To hang on the tree" thus means either crucifixion or execution by hanging on a pole. Earlier it was held that crucifixion was the capital punishment of the gentiles, never of the Jews. (Crucifixion was invented by the Persians, then taken over by Alexander the Great and his successors, among them the Syrians, and later the Romans). It has therefore been argued that the fact that Jesus was crucified demonstrates that his death was the responsibility of the Romans, not of the Jews. The cry of the Jewish mob that is quoted in the Gospels "Crucify him!" is therefore viewed as unhistoric. As good Jews they should have shouted "Have him killed!" or "Have him stoned," but not "Crucify him!"

The Israeli scholar Yigael Yadin, who deciphered and published the Temple Scroll some years ago, changed these presuppositions. Yadin and others, for example the well known Catholic scholar, J.M. Fitzmyer, have shown that the Temple Scroll reflects a *Jewish* priestly *halakhah* from the early second century BC to the fall of the Temple, which ordains that the one who is guilty of national treason or blasphemy shall die by being hanged upon the tree. (The phrase "for those who hang on the tree are accursed by God and men" has the double meaning "curse God" and "be accursed by God"). A sinner of this kind should be killed in the most awesome way, by being hanged on the tree before his people (whom he has betrayed) and before God (whom he has blasphemed). And while he is hanging on the tree he is, according to the word of the Torah, accursed by God and men. Indications of this theology are found both in rabbinical literature and early Aramaic translations of the Bible (*Targumim Jonathan* and *Neofyti* to Numbers 25:4. Targum to Ruth 1:17). Not only the Essenes held this position, but probably also the other priestly group, the Sadducees, those who were the party in power in the days of Jesus.

Crucifixion and the Jews

History shows that on a few occasions crucifixion or execution by hanging on the tree was indeed practiced by Jews. Joshua executed the King of Ai by hanging him (alive) on a tree (Joshua 8:29). Crucifixion probably became Jewish custom in the Maccabean period, influenced by the practice of the Seleucid overlords in Syria. Antiochus Epiphanes used crucifixion in his persecution of Torah-obedient Jews in Judea. In 162BC the high priest Alcimus had 60 pious Jews executed by crucifixion, among them the priestly scribe Jose ben Joezer (1 Maccabees 7:16; *Genesis Rabbah* 65:22, which uses the Hebrew verb for crucify). In the aftermath of a revolt in 90BC in which the Pharisees allied themselves with the Syrians (cf. the phrase "delivers his people to the gentiles and performs evil on his people"), King Alexander Janneus crucified 800 Pharisees in Jerusalem. Another Qumran scroll, the commentary on the book of Nahum (The scholarly designation is 4QpNah I 6–8), lauds Janneus for this deed, which followed the priestly tradition of law. This commentary comments on the lion of Nahum 2:13. Parts of the text are missing, but it should probably be reconstructed: "Its interpretation concerns the furious young lion (Janneus) who [found] those seeking smooth things (the Pharisees) [guilty of a crime punishable by death] and hanged men alive [on the tree for such is the law] in Israel from before." Two decades later, the leader of the Sanhedrin, Shimon ben Shetah, had 80 witches from Ashkelon hanged on the tree (Mishnah *Sanhedrin* 6:4. The Jerusalem Talmud, *Hagiga* 11:2).

In this light the cry "Crucify him" is exactly what we should expect of the Sadducean leaders, "the chief priests and their officials" (John 19:6). The high priest had torn his garments when he heard Jesus talking about himself as the heavenly Son of Man seated on God's right hand: "He has spoken blasphemy!" After Jesus raised Lazarus from the dead the Sadducean high priests viewed Jesus as a threat against the Temple and the people (John 11:46–50). And they, the chiefs of the temple, certainly perceived Jesus' word that he could rebuild the Temple in three days (John 2:19) as blasphemy or national treason. Consequently, they deemed him as one who should be hanged on the tree. According to political reality, this had to be implemented by the Roman rulers of the land. When it was not in their own power to hang the blasphemer on the tree, they pressured Pilate to do it. It is historically incorrect to make the Jewish people as such responsible for the execution of Jesus; those responsible were the Sadducean temple leadership together with the Roman authorities.

A Messiah should not hang on a cross, accursed by God and men. Therefore some of those passing by the cross of Jesus mocked "He is the King of Israel. Let him come down now from the cross!" The one who was crucified and cursed could not have been the Messiah.

Peter knows this paradox when he boldly tells the Sanhedrin, the Jewish Council, that "the God of our fathers raised Jesus from the dead — whom you had killed by hanging him on the tree" (Acts 5:30). So does Paul who "preaches a crucified Messiah, a stumbling block to Jews and foolishness to gentiles" (1 Corinthians 1:23). And in Galatians 3:13 he puts forward a daring claim: "The Messiah redeemed us from the curse of the Torah by becoming a curse for us, for it is written: 'Cursed is everyone who is hung on a tree.'" Paul, raised as a Pharisee in Jerusalem, knew the priestly doctrine of his days. He knew that Jesus hung accursed on the cross. But the rabbi from Tarsus provides a new interpretation. He knows that God has raised the accursed from the dead and thereby demonstrated that he is the Messiah. This fact means that the curse Jesus carried on the cross was not his own; it was ours. And by willingly taking the curse of the Torah on our behalf, he redeems both Israelites and gentiles from the curse which befell us all because we did not manage to obey the Torah. Redemption is at hand!

A Rabbinical Parable

One of the famous rabbis of the second century AD, Rabbi Meir, used a parable in order to explain the difficult verse from Deuteronomy:

> "Anyone who is hung on a tree is accursed by God." Why was he hanged? Because he blasphemed the name of God. Rabbi Meir equals this with two identical twins who were living in the same city, one was righteous and the other was a scoundrel. The first was made king of the city. When his brother committed robbery, the king ordered him to be hanged on the tree. But when he heard that all those passing by the executed shouted in distress: "The king is hanging on the tree," he ordered the body to be taken down. Thus we learn that when men feel sorry at such a sight, even more does God Himself who says: "What a disgrace this is for Me, because man is my progeny." There-

fore Scripture says: anyone who is hung on a tree is under God's curse (*Midrash Tannaim* to Deuteronomy 21:23. The Babylonian Talmud, *Sanhedrin* 46b).

The citizens saw the image of their king hanging on the tree. Man is God's image — this is true also for the unrighteous. When we see an executed man hanging on the tree, we see the image of the Great King hanging there. And such a blasphemous disgrace cannot be tolerated for long, therefore the body must be taken down before evening.

I dare to apply a new interpretation to Rabbi Meir's parable: Not only does everyone hanged on the tree represent God's image, one of those thousands hanged on a cross by the Romans represented God's image *par excellence.* "He is the radiance of God's glory and the representation of his nature" (Hebrews 1:3). When we see him on the cross we see the image of the Great King — of the divine Messiah who took the curse of mankind upon himself to bring redemption to Jew and gentile alike.

6

The Messiah Who Died For Our Sins

Sam Nadler

It may seem strange and confusing to some to understand the message of the New Covenant in light of modern discussions regarding national and global needs and expectations of what a hero or Messiah should do. After all, even if I do have many personal needs, how does this measure against hunger, war, natural disasters, etc.? Why should God so greatly care about my apparently inconsequential sins and minor difficulties that he would send the Messiah, whose apparent first order of business is not in bringing peace to the world, but in securing me for heaven?

Not incidentally, this is precisely what the New Covenant states: that Messiah Yeshua (Jesus) suffered and died for sins, not merely as a martyr or hero, but as an atonement for "all who will believe."

The New Covenant Proclamation of the Messiah

The New Covenant is replete with evidence for a suffering Savior. Notice the following statements made by Yeshua himself and Jewish witnesses about the one who claimed to be the Jewish Messiah:

> Messiah should suffer and rise again from the dead the third day; and that repentance for forgiveness of sins should be proclaimed in His name (Luke 24:46, 47).

> For God so loved the world, that He gave His only begotten Son, that whoever believes in Him should not perish, but have eternal life (John 3:16).

> He...was delivered up because of our transgressions (Romans 4:25).

> ...while we were enemies, we were reconciled to God through the death of His Son (Romans 5:10).

> ... that Messiah died for our sins according to the Scriptures (1 Corinthians 15:3).

Much more could be added from the New Covenant record and it is worth the effort to get the New Testament and read the following references: Matthew 20:28; John 3:14, 15; 10:11; Acts 8:32–35; 10:39, 40, 43; 13:28–30, 38; Romans 3:24, 25; 5:8; 8:32, 34; 1 Corinthians 1:18; 8:11; 2 Corinthians 5:15, 18–21; Galatians 1:3, 4; 2:20; 3:13; 4:4–5; Ephesians 1:7; 2:13, 16; 5:2, 26; Colossians 1:14, 20, 22; 1 Timothy 1:15; 2:6; Titus 2:14; 3:4–6; Hebrews 5:8–9; 7:25–27; 9:14, 26, 28; 10:10, 12, 14, 19–20; 13:12; 1 Peter 1:3, 18, 19; 2:24; 3:18; 1 John 2:2; 3:16; 4:10; Revelation 1:5; 5:9; 7:14, 15; 12:11.

The next question we will look at is this: Is the message of a suffering Messiah authoritatively Jewish?

The Torah's Promise for Israel

As we look to the foundation of all Jewish authority, the Tanakh, the Scriptures, which Christians call the Old Testament, we see clear evidence that the New Covenant message of reconciliation to God through the sacrifice of the Messiah is indeed authoritatively Jewish. For the whole Torah — i.e. the Law and the Jewish Scriptures in their entirety — is laid out in such a way as to show us the Law as God's holy standard and, as such, the impossibility of keeping it perfectly. But a way to God is presented in the Law that does not circumvent God's holy requirements, but rather acknowledges them: the Jewish sacrificial system.

Israel's Need for a Sacrifice

From the beginning of Torah, blood sacrifices as covering and atonement were required (Genesis 3:12; 4:4). When finally the Law was given at Sinai, intrinsic to that Law was the sacrificial system needed to maintain a relationship between a Holy God and a less than holy, though humble, people. For the Law was not given to demonstrate man's ability to attain righteousness through obedience. Rather, the Law was to show man's inability to be holy and to reveal God's mercy and grace as the only means of establishing and sustaining a relationship with the Lord.

And so, Yom Kippur (the Day of Atonement) is predicated upon a blood sacrifice (Leviticus 16:3–27; 23:27). Thus when Scripture says in Leviticus 16:30 and 34

> for it is on this day that atonement shall be made for you to cleanse you; you shall be clean from all your sins before the Lord...and now you shall have this as a permanent statute, to make atonement for the sons of Israel for all their sins once every year....

it is in the context of a blood sacrifice for sins, and not merely with repentance and "humbling" of our souls. In fact, every area of sin, both intentional and unintentional (Leviticus 4:2), both of attitude and of action (Leviticus 5:1), was atoned for by a blood sacrifice.

Even in one's poverty, if one were too poor to afford a blood sacrifice, and could only afford some flour for a sin offering, still it was placed "on the altar, *with* the offerings of the Lord" (Leviticus 5:12). Although not containing blood, it was placed *upon* and identified *with* the blood offering, making *it* a blood offering and appropriate.

Even when away from the Land and the Temple, even through exile because of sin, if God's people will pray toward "the house," the Temple, the place of sacrifice (2 Chronicles 7:12), God will hear their prayer for they are identifying with the sacrifice upon the altar, even if the altar and Temple are gone (1 Kings 8:46–50). Daniel so prayed "toward Jerusalem" (Daniel 6:10) to fulfill "the law of his God" (6:5) and to identify with the blood altar.

Where I grew up, at our home, we ate our meat "orthodox style," that is, well done, without blood. This practice comes from Leviticus 17:10–14, which states blood is not for eating; rather it has a different purpose:

> The life of the flesh is in the blood, and I have given it to you on the altar to make atonement for your souls; for it is the blood by reason of the life that makes atonement (Leviticus 17:11).

There is, therefore, no atonement without the blood offering. "But, why," one might ask, "is a blood sacrifice necessary?" The answer is: "Sin."

The Seriousness of Sin

To us, sin may not seem all that horrendous, but to God sin offends and contradicts his holy character and cuts off the individual sinner from a relationship with him. The sin becomes like a debt that the individual can never pay, like breaking a Ming vase that is irreplaceable...and too expensive to ever pay back.

And the sin against God is even more, and eternally, costly. Thus, our eternal souls alone will pay the debt of sin. That is why God states emphatically, "The soul that sins, it shall die"...forever

(Ezekiel 18:4).

Not only does sin have an eternal effect, but it also has the immediate effect of breaking our intimacy and personal communication with God:

> Behold, the Lord's hand is not so short that it cannot save; neither is His ear so dull that it cannot hear. But your iniquities have made a separation between you and your God, and your sins have hidden His face from you, so that He does not hear…(Isaiah 59:1, 2).

That means that as much as one might want God to answer a prayer about health, for example, and as much as God might desire to answer prayer as well, it goes unanswered because of a greater issue that needs to be dealt with: Sin.

It would be silly for someone who robbed me to come and ask for a favor, like a loan or gift, for I would say, "How can we even discuss a favor, until we settle the difficulty between us!" Thus it is with God. He cannot and will not deal with the many favors and blessings we desire, and he desires to give us, until the sin issue is settled. And the only way it is settled is by sacrifice. Sacrifice for both the immediate and eternal consequences of sin.

So all through the Torah the issue of sin and sacrifice was a major theme. But also, and along with this, was another and even more significant theme: Messiah.

The Sacrifice of the Messiah

When sin first dealt its deadly blow, we see the first mention of the one who would finally deal with sin (Genesis 3:15). This one is recognized in traditional circles as Messiah (*Genesis Rabbah* 12; *Numbers Rabbah* 13; and of course the Targumim to these passages). Thus, although we see sin dealt with immediately (although temporarily) by a blood sacrifice on the altar, the ultimate and final solution to the problem of sin is found in the Messiah. This is most fully stated by Isaiah the prophet (c. 700BC) in 52:13–53:12. The fullness of this portion should be seen in its entirety, so that we may appreciate the full measure of God's comprehensive handling of the sin/separation problem:

> [13]Behold, My servant will prosper. He will be high and lifted up, and greatly exalted. [14]Just as many were astonished at you, My People, so His appearance was marred more than any man, and His form more than the sons of men. [15]Thus He will sprinkle many nations. Kings will shut their mouths on account of Him; for what had not been told them they will see, and what they had not heard they will understand.
>
> [1]Who has believed our message? And to whom has the arm of the Lord been revealed? [2]For He grew up before Him like a tender shoot, and like a root out of parched ground; He has no stately form or majesty that we should look upon Him, nor appearance that we should be attracted to Him. [3]He was despised and forsaken of men, a man of sorrows, and acquainted with grief; and like one from whom men hide their face, He was despised, and we did not esteem Him.
>
> [4]Surely our griefs He Himself bore, and our sorrows He carried; yet we ourselves esteemed Him stricken, smitten of God, and afflicted. [5]But He was pierced through for our transgressions, He was crushed for our iniquities; the chastening for our well-being fell upon Him, and by His scourging we are healed. [6]All of us like sheep have gone astray, each of us has turned to his own way; but the Lord has caused the iniquity of us all to fall on Him.
>
> [7]He was oppressed and He was afflicted. Yet He did not open His mouth; like a lamb that is led to slaughter, and like a sheep that is silent before its shearers, so He did not open His mouth. [8]By oppression and judgment He was taken away; and as for His generation, who considered that He was cut off out of the land of the living, for the transgression of My people to whom the stroke

was due? [9]His grave was assigned with wicked men, yet He was with a rich man in His death, because He had done no violence, nor was there any deceit in His mouth. [10]But the Lord was pleased to crush Him, putting Him to grief; if He would render Himself as a guilt offering, He will see His offspring, He will prolong His days, and the good pleasure of the Lord will prosper in His hand. [11]As a result of the anguish of His soul, He will see it and be satisfied; by His knowledge the Righteous One, My Servant, will justify the many, as He will bear their iniquities. [12]Therefore, I will allot Him a portion with the great, and He will divide the booty with the strong; because He poured out Himself to death, and was numbered with the transgressors; yet He Himself bore the sin of many, and interceded for the transgressors.

This portion of Scripture was recognized as referring to Messiah even in ancient Jewish tradition: *Targumim Jonathan* (Ben Uzziel) on Isaiah 52:13 says, "Behold, My servant the Messiah shall prosper, he shall be exalted and great and very powerful"; it is also according to The Babylonian Talmud, *Sanhedrin* 98a, b; and Isaac Abrabanel (1437–1508) states that the "majority of the Midrashim" agree.

As we observe that the portion is in three sections, or movements, please note that in 52:13–15, God is speaking; in 53:1–9, Israel is speaking; and in 53:10–12, God speaks in conclusion. In the first section, God says that his Servant would be greatly exalted (52:13) despite the great suffering he would incur (52:14). This suffering would be the greatest suffering of any person. This would be hard to understand, until we see farther down that the sufferings would include bearing the sins of his people (53:6). Thus, as the New Covenant words it, "He made Him who knew no sin [to be] sin [offering] on our behalf" (2 Corinthians 5:21). And so his suffering was "more than any man."

And the sufferer's ultimate impact would be global. Kings, not from a Jewish frame of reference, and therefore untaught (or untold), would be "sprinkled" (as in sanctified by a blood offering, cf. Exodus 24:6–8). Thus, non-Jewish kings would be positively impacted by the blood offering of Messiah (cf. a similar thought in Isaiah 49:7). The Servant, the Messiah, would suffer, and that suffering would not keep him from being exalted but would, in fact, influence the nations of the world.

In the second section (53:1–9, where Israel is speaking) we see that the suffering of the Servant/Messiah was a heavenly paradox. The suffering would, on the one hand, be for the benefit of Israel ("with His chastening we are healed," "the Lord has caused the iniquity of us all to fall on Him," etc.). But on the other hand, the suffering itself would be interpreted by Israel as a reason not to acknowledge the Sufferer as the Servant of God/Messiah!

- In 53:1–3, the Sufferer is too ordinary in appearance to be taken seriously.
- In 53:4–6, the Sufferer endures far too much punishment for the people to identify with him.
- In 53:7–9, the Sufferer is far too submissive, and therefore is thought to be accepting the punishment as due him (although he is voluntarily surrendering himself as a substitutionary offering for Israel — and whoever else would believe the report, 53:1; 52:15).

In fact, the final stanzas (53:10–12) make it perfectly clear that he himself would be the trespass offering that would satisfy the holy demands of a Holy God (53:11). In fact, the Sufferer would be rewarded not despite the suffering, but because of it ("Because He poured out Himself to death," v. 12).

This section from Isaiah clearly shows the Jewish perspective on the awfulness of sin, satisfied only by the blood sacrifice fulfilled completely in the Messiah.

Thus, the New Covenant Presentation of Yeshua

Because of the Torah's theme (that of man's sinful condition and the need for a blood sacrifice), and its promise (of that sacri-

fice being fulfilled in Messiah), we can therefore see the fulfillment of the Jewish Scriptures in the theme of the New Covenant: the Messiah who died for our sins. This alone is the biblical, and therefore the totally authoritative, Jewish view.

The story, though, doesn't end with Messiah's death. For even
in Isaiah 53, we see clear indications that Messiah would not stay
dead! For He would "prolong His days," "see His seed," receive
his reward and be exalted.

Yes, the New Covenant record is true. Yeshua the Messiah
died as the final atonement for our sins, and was raised from the
dead. Thus, Yeshua alone has fulfilled all the Torah, as well as the
lives of all who will "believe the report" — and trust in him.

7

The Risen Messiah: Firstfruits of the Resurrection

Barry A. Rubin

But the fact is that the Messiah has been raised from the dead, the firstfruits of those who have died (I Corinthians 15:20).

What was Firstfruits?

To grasp the full meaning of Paul's words, one needs to understand the Feast of Firstfruits, an important biblical holiday.

The Lord spoke to Moses, "Speak to the Israelites and say to them: 'When you enter the land I am going to give you and you reap its harvest, bring to the priest a sheaf of the first grain you harvest. He is to wave the sheaf before the Lord so it will be accepted on your behalf; the priest is to wave it on the day after the

Sabbath.... This is to be a lasting ordinance for the generations to come, wherever you live.

From the day after the Sabbath, the day you brought the sheaf of the wave offering, count off seven full weeks. Count off fifty days up to the day after the seventh Sabbath, and then present an offering of new grain to the Lord...a wave offering of firstfruits to the Lord.'" (Leviticus 23:9–11, 14b–17).

Most Bibles indicate a separation between these two firstfruit observances, and rightly so. Two distinct holidays are described. However, the Lord connected them by instructing his people to perform a special counting, "the counting of the days of the omer," between the two observances. Being aware of this is important to our understanding of Paul's use of the expression, "firstfruits."

Israel, especially ancient Israel, was an agricultural land. The people were vitally connected to the land and its produce. Because of this, so they would remember from where their blessings came, the Lord instructed them to return to him an offering of thanksgiving when they reaped a harvest.

When was Firstfruits?

The *first* firstfruit offering took place during Passover week, "the day after the Sabbath." Controversy surrounds whether the "Sabbath" referred to is the sabbath-day of Passover (actually, the first day of the Feast of Unleavened Bread) or the seventh-day-of-the-week Sabbath. The Pharisees taught that the Lord was referring to the former, a sabbath day (Leviticus 23:7), and began counting the days of the omer on the day after that Sabbath. The Sadducees believed the verse referred to the seventh-day-of-the-week Sabbath.

According to the renowned Jewish historian, Josephus, the prevailing position was that of the Pharisees:

But on the second day of unleavened bread, which is the sixteenth day of the month, they first partake of the fruits of the earth.... And while they suppose it proper to honour God, from whom they obtain this plentiful provision in the first place, they offer the firstfruits of their barley ... (Josephus, *Antiquities of the Jews,* Book III, Chapter 10, Paragraph 5.)

To this day, Jews who count the days of the omer begin the fifty-day count after the first day of Passover, a sabbath day. According to Theodore Gaster, who expounds this viewpoint in *Festivals of the Jewish Year*:

The counting, which commences on the second night of Passover, is performed in a ceremonial fashion every evening at sunset. It is prefaced by a blessing recalling the Biblical ordinance, and is followed by the recitation of the Sixty-seventh Psalm ("The earth hath yielded her produce; God, our own God, is blessing us.") A prayer is also offered for the rebuilding of the Temple and the restoration of the ancient services.

The Omer Days are observed as a kind of Lent. At least during the earlier portion of them, it is not permitted to solemnize marriages, cut the hair, wear new clothes, listen to music or attend any form of public entertainment.

Various explanations are given to this custom of self-denial, but considering the fact that the Feast of Firstfruits is organically connected to the next holiday, *Shavuot,* the Feast of Weeks, or Pentecost, when the barley harvest is finished, we understand the desire to relate these two important holidays.

Getting back to the question of what Sabbath was in mind when the ordinances for observance were given, a close examination of the biblical texts cited above shows that the Sadducees were correct. It is true that they did not believe in the resurrection of the dead, but that would not impact when they began their fifty-day count. The biblically correct day on which to begin counting was the day after the seventh-day Sabbath of

Passover week. Fifty days from that day brings us to another "day after the Sabbath," the *second* firstfruits offering. Since *Shavuot,* Pentecost, came on the day after a Sabbath, then counting back seven weeks brings one to another "day after a Sabbath," indicating that the first Firstfruits should begin on the first day of the week.

As we know, Messiah was raised from the dead after the seventh-day Sabbath that came during his last Passover week, strengthening the argument for the Sadducean position on which to begin the counting of the omer. Might it be possible that, in order to mitigate against the reality of the resurrection of Yeshua (Jesus), the Pharisee's position became pre-eminent? Most of the Pharisees, the religious leaders of their day, rejected the Messiahship of Yeshua.

The Reality of the Resurrection

Whenever the counting commenced, however, the fact of the resurrection was a message of which Paul was persuaded. Paul, raised in the Pharisaic school, knew the reality of resurrection. He had been trained to believe that when Abraham willingly agreed to sacrifice his son, Isaac, at the Lord's request, the Lord would bring him back to life. That's why the writer to the Messianic Jews, the Hebrew believers, wrote, "For he [Abraham] had concluded that God could raise people from the dead!" (Hebrews 11:19). Paul believed this truth.

He also accepted the affirmation of the Psalmist, "But God will redeem my soul from the grave; he will surely take me to himself" (Psalm 49:15). He believed the words of Job, "I know that my redeemer lives, and that in the end he will stand upon the earth. And after my skin has been destroyed, yet in my flesh I will see God" (Job 19:25–26). Paul trusted the teaching expressed by Isaiah: "But your dead will live; their bodies will rise. You who dwell in the dust, wake up and shout for joy....the earth will give birth to her dead" (Isaiah 26:19). He affirmed the truths of Ezekiel, "O my people, I am going to open your graves and bring you up from them....Then you, my people, will know that I am the Lord, when I open your graves and bring you up from them" (Ezekiel 37:12–13).

Paul understood that if the resurrection of the Messiah was a myth, then his faith was in vain. He had based his trust in Messiah on the entire *Tanakh* (the Old Testament) as well as the person of Yeshua. In response to some who were saying that there was no resurrection, Paul wrote:

> But if it has been proclaimed that the Messiah has been raised from the dead, how is it that some of you are saying there is no such thing as a resurrection of the dead? If there is no resurrection of the dead, then the Messiah has not been raised; and if the Messiah has not been raised, then what we have proclaimed is in vain; also your trust is in vain...For if the dead are not raised, then the Messiah has not been raised either; and if the Messiah has not been raised, your trust is useless, and you are still in your sins...But the fact is that the Messiah has been raised from the dead, the firstfruits of those who have died (I Corinthians 15:12–14, 16–17, 20).

Keeping in mind that the Jews of his day practiced two firstfruits holidays, it is apparent that Paul was relating the resurrection of Yeshua to the biblical concept of firstfruits.

The Hope of the Resurrection

The *first* firstfruits foretold that there would be *latter* fruits, for if there were little barley harvest, the earliest agricultural harvest, then it would be unlikely that there would be much of a latter harvest. If the early rains did not provide water for the growth of barley, then the ground would be too dry for other crops to come. In a sense, harvesting the firstfruits and offering them to God was like a down-payment on good crops yet to come.

Paul must have had this in mind when he continued his thoughts about resurrection:

For since death came through a man, also the resurrection of the dead has come through a man. For just as in connection with Adam all die, so in connection with the Messiah all will be made alive. But each in his own order: the Messiah is the firstfruits; then those who belong to the Messiah, at the time of his coming; then the culmination, when he hands over the Kingdom to God the Father.... It will take but a moment, the blink of an eye, at the final shofar [ram's horn]. For the shofar will sound, and the dead will be raised to live forever, and we too will be changed...then this passage in the Tanakh will be fulfilled: "Death is swallowed up in victory" (I Corinthians 15:21–24, 52, 54).

The ultimate harvest is the resurrection of all mankind, "some," as Daniel wrote, "to everlasting life, others to shame and everlasting contempt" (12:2). Those who have put their trust in the savior of Israel, Yeshua, the Messiah, will be raised to everlasting life, for it is written, "For God so loved the world that he gave his only and unique son, so that everyone who trusts in him may have eternal life, instead of being utterly destroyed" (John 3:16). But eternal life begins with the *firstfruits* of the resurrection. If we don't trust the fact of history that Yeshua literally rose from the dead, how can we expect to be included in the blessings that come from the latter resurrection?

When we meditate upon the resurrection of the Messiah during Passover season, we, like the Jews of Yeshua's day, can affirm with the Psalmist, "The earth has yielded her produce; God, our own God, is blessing us." Yeshua, "firstfruits of the resurrection," paves the way for the latter resurrection and eternal life, the greatest blessing anyone can have.

8

Jewish Christianity— The First Century

Arthur F. Glasser

It is the year 100CE. A group of Jewish followers of Jesus has gathered in Jerusalem to reflect on the changing status of Jewish Christianity as the century draws to an end. Who are they? A few of them might remember the Apostolic Age when the steadily growing Christian movement was largely Jewish. A larger number might be able to recall with vividness the outreach into the gentile world spear-headed by Paul, prior to the Great Revolt. But the majority would be members of the post-war generation. Although they would doubtless be encouraged by the spectacular gains the Church was making among gentiles throughout the Mediterranean world, they would be primarily concerned over their own future in the land of Israel. Was another revolt brewing? What follows are the main contributions that Jewish believers made to the larger Christian movement during the first century and the external factors that shaped their own life and witness.

The Great Revolt (66–73CE)

Initially, it was a popular uprising, but it ended in total defeat for all Jewry. Jerusalem, Temple and the Land! — all had been reduced to rubble by the Romans in ruthless response to the revolt precipitated by the Zealots. Yes, there were grievances, and the Zealots believed they were honoring God, fully expecting that he would intervene. But God did not come to their rescue, and more than 600,000 Jews were slaughtered, almost a quarter of the total Jewish population of Palestine. The followers of Jesus escaped, because he had earlier told them: "When you see Jerusalem surrounded by armies, then know that its desolation has come near. Then let those who are in Judea flee to the mountains, and let those who are inside the city depart, and let not those who are out in the country enter it… Jerusalem will be trodden down by the Gentiles" (Luke 21:20, 21, 24). In obedience, thousands of Jewish Christians emigrated from Jerusalem to Pella in Transjordan. Years later, when they returned, all was devastation — and so unnecessarily so!

Whereas the triumph of the Roman Emperor Titus marked the virtual end of Palestinian Jewry, his destruction of Jerusalem not only confirmed the prophetic authority of Jesus but vindicated his Messiahship. The city which had crucified its Messiah was stripped of its symbolic significance as the central Jewish stronghold of reaction and the rabbinic preoccupation with the Law.

Positive Achievements

Attention should first be given to the positive and commanding influence that Jewish Christianity exercised on the larger gentile Christian movement prior to the war. From that first Pentecost when the Church was born it was almost exclusively Jews through whom God revealed his Word in the form of 27 books (the New Testament). And it was they who also promoted the cruciality of adhering to the Apostles' doctrine (Acts 2:42). They also demanded loyalty to the Jewish roots of the "New Covenant" faith. This ensured that the New Testament be understood only by constant reflection on the Old Testament. It is significant that during the post-war period when Jewish Christians were being increasingly separated from all social linkage with their people, they remained insistent that the Old Testament be retained as the larger segment of the total Christian Bible. During those early decades following the emergence of the Christian movement at Pentecost (the Feast of Shavuot, 30CE), Jewish believers had no intention of separating themselves from their own people. Indeed, when Paul visited Jerusalem toward the end of his ministry in the Eastern Mediterranean he was met by church leaders who said: "You see, brother, how many thousands there are among the Jews of those who have believed; they are all zealous for the Law" (Acts 21:20). This was largely the pattern before the Jewish-Roman war. Messianic Jews participated in temple services and together with all Jews worshiped in the synagogues, practiced circumcision, observed Sabbath and other holy days, along with *kashrut* (the Jewish Dietary laws), and respected the high priest as was befitting "observant Jews" (23:2–5).

Just before the Jewish-Roman war, the letter to the Hebrews was written and distributed. It called attention to the fact that with Messiah's issuance of the New Covenant and redemptive sacrifice of himself on the cross, the Levitical economy mandated at Sinai had been fulfilled, and replaced. The destruction of the Temple shortly thereafter and the dissolution of the priesthood likewise confirmed this and took on eschatological significance. God had brought all visible elements of the old economy to an end as a judgment against Israel's persistent "No!" to Jesus, the Messiah. But more, this letter provided Jesus' followers with insight into his high priestly work. As the Messiah he entered "once for all into the Holy Place, taking… his own blood, and thus securing an eternal redemption for both Israel and the nations" (9:11–12). "He abolished the first in order to establish the second" (10:9). It was Jewish Christians who first understood their Messianic faith to be the continuation of the great themes of biblical Judaism, and utterly consistent with its ancient traditions.

In addition, it was Jewish Christians who made a significant contribution to the universality of the Christian movement. They accomplished this not only by their prophetic emphasis on God working and revealing his will in the circumstances of human history. By sharing the gospel with the gentiles, they underscored the relevance of the Old Testament appeals of God to the whole human race: "Turn to Me and be saved, all the ends of the earth! For I am God, and there is no other" (Isaiah 45:22).

The Jewish "Advantage"

Admittedly, Jewish Christianity contributed greatly to the self-understanding of the Church. Actually, its list of contributions far exceeds the items mentioned above, and this is inevitable. The Hebrew people occupy a unique position in biblical revelation. But although Paul argues that all peoples are without distinction before God (Romans 3:22) and that no one people can boast or claim privileges (3:9), he argued that there is an advantage to being a Jew ("much in every way", 3:1, 2). This followed because of their unique election to be a "light to the nations" (Isaiah 49:6). Never has there been a people that has undergone such suffering and humiliation. By all expectations they should have disintegrated and disappeared. However, even after their appalling suffering during the Great Revolt, particularly in the siege of Jerusalem, the Jews as a people remained unbroken in spirit, conscious of their dignity and still retaining a sense of mission and purpose. Had Paul not written his letter to the Romans and inquired into "the advantage of the Jews," gentile Christians would have believed that the Jews' usefulness to God and his worldwide mission had come to an end with their rejection of Jesus. But Paul speaks of their future service on behalf of the nation as "life from the dead" when they are "grafted back into their own olive tree" (11:24).

Jewish Messianic Disunity

In the year 100CE Jewish Christians in Palestine were still disturbed by residual elements of a controversy that had broken out in their midst 50 years before. At that time some "Jewish believers who belonged to the party of the Pharisees insisted that gentile converts be circumcised and charged to keep the law of Moses" (Acts 15:1, 5). This issue was initially so formidable and threatening that a special council was convened in Jerusalem to deal with it. After much debate James reconciled the disparate positions when he formulated the following decision: "It is my judgment that we should not trouble those Gentiles who turn to God, but should write to them to abstain from the pollutions of idols and from unchastity and from what is strangled and from blood" (15:19, 20). Though spared circumcision, gentile believers were expected to adhere to some of the limitations of Jewish dietary laws. Jewish believers remained free to continue to practice circumcision and live according to the Law of Moses. Naturally, all hoped that these concessions would end the controversy.

But this was not to be. The subsequent history of Jewish Christianity was replete with much argument and schism over this matter. When a Jewish person accepted Jesus as Lord and Savior, not all were agreed as to how his or her Jewishness was to be expressed. Should the rabbinic interpretation of the Law be followed, though not with the Pharasaic understanding of making oneself thereby fit for the Presence of God? Or should one seek to demonstrate the reality of which the Apostle Paul spoke when he declared that the Messiah became "the end of the Law for righteousness" for all true believers (Romans 10:4)? Some argued that the destruction of the Temple, along with the end of the Levitical priesthood and cult, made this whole matter a non-issue. But the debate continued, and by the year 100CE Jewish Christianity was beginning to fracture.

Unprecedented Growth

Inevitably the destruction of the Temple, the failure of military action to bring about national liberation, and the almost complete survival of the Messianic Jewish community that had sought in every way to retain its status within Jewry were factors that together gave the followers of Jesus an enormous appeal to non-establishment Jews. But not to the rabbis.

They were concerned that too many Jewish people were coming to faith in Jesus. Something had to be done to check further erosion from the Synagogue. Because most Jews were not yet ready to regard Jesus of Nazareth as the promised Messiah, those who gathered for synagogue worship decided to make it uncomfortable for Messianic Jews to attend. But how could they accomplish this without resorting to some form of violent excommunication?

It was Rabbi Samuel the Little who suggested that a malediction be inserted in the Amidah, the ancient series of liturgical prayers popular in the synagogue in those days. This became known as *Birkat ha-minim* (the 12th Benediction: Against Heretics). This malediction called down on the *Minim* or Messianic Jews a curse that stripped them of all hope in the world to come because of their belief that the Messiah had already appeared on earth. One can readily imagine the sense of total ostracism that the Messianic Jews experienced when their turn came to lead in the *Amidah* recitation. They would certainly stumble over having to call down a curse on the *Minim* — their own brothers and sisters in the faith. What could they do but sadly withdraw from all synagogue life?

Conclusion

Such is the record of a particular group of Jewish people as they looked back over the tumultuous first century of the Christian era and faced with real foreboding the century to follow. They possessed the unique distinction of being the privileged people through whom God entered human history via the Incarnation and by whom the biblical faith of his people was shaped. And it was through their apostolic witness that the knowledge of the God of Abraham, Isaac and Jacob first became accessible to the whole human race.

9

The Messianic Idea in Judaism

Louis Goldberg

The Middle Ages and its Heritage

Maimonides, also called the Rambam (1135–1204), has 13 principles of faith in his Commentary on the Mishnah, the introduction to Mishnah *Sanhedrin* 10:1. The 12th principle states:

> I believe with a complete faith in the coming of the Messiah; and even though he tarry, nevertheless I await him every day that he should come.

He further expands his belief in the Messiah in his *Mishnah Torah* ("The Second Torah"), by stating that when he does come, he does not have to perform signs and wonders, nor bring new things in the world. Neither will he change the customary order of this world or bring about something new in the order of creation.

Traditional Judaism also has a concept of a second Messiah, son of Joseph, and some find this concept to be based on the interpretation of Obadiah, "The house of Jacob will be a fire and the house of Joseph a flame; the house of Esau will be stubble and they will set them on fire and consume them" (v. 18). This belief appears to be in place, either by the end of the Tannaim period, which closed with the production in 200CE of the Mishnah, or for sure in the early 200's, in the Amoraim period. No doubt, the Rambam was aware of this belief.

The Jewish traditional teaching in Rambam's day was in a Messiah who is personal, the son of David, who will yet come to institute a kingdom of peace. They still followed the Targumic paraphrase on Isaiah 53 which possibly already existed orally by the end of the Second Temple Period. In it, all passages which spoke of suffering were relegated to Israel as the suffering servant, while the verses which spoke of exaltation were applied to the Messiah, son of David.

A Contrary View

Already, however, some disquieting notes were being registered in the Middle Ages. In Ibn Ezra's (1092?–1168) commentary on the Hebrew Scriptures and particularly on Isaiah 53, Israel is regarded as the servant of the Lord and therefore, the entire chapter refers to the nation. The "man of sorrows" (Isaiah 53:3), is "the servant of the Lord, or the whole nation of the Israelites." Ibn Ezra describes the reference to suffering as "the troubles which Israel has to suffer during the exile."

David Baron, a Jewish believer in the early part of this century, suggested that when Ibn Ezra wrote his commentary on the Talmud, he followed the older interpretation which applied the exaltation passages of Isaiah 53 to a Messiah who is personal. However, he probably wrote his commentary on the Bible, including Isaiah, after the Second Crusade when so many Jewish people were massacred in Europe.

Once the door was open, however, that Isaiah 53 could refer to the entire nation and not to any Messiah who is personal, it then became easier for Jews to deny that this one chapter graphically describes Yeshua (Jesus) as the Messiah. For centuries, many in Christendom have used this testimony of Isaiah; but Jewish people now possessed a good tool for their defense against the claims for the Messiah from Isaiah 53 who suffers and dies for our sins.

Other Jewish exegetes quickly picked up on Ibn Ezra's work and Baron refers to the exposition by Manasseh ben Israel (1604–1657), *Reconciliation*, which refers much of Isaiah 53 to Israel. For example, the passage "My righteous servant shall justify many" describes Israel as the righteous people who will justify many by their knowledge and wisdom. Israel will bring many to the true religion; through their suffering, they will be the example to all nations.

By and large, however, traditional Jewish people, particularly during the Middle Ages, clung to the older understanding. Father Flannery in *The Anguish of the Jews*, a chronicle of Jewish suffering through the centuries, describes this people, by the 1500's as "terrorized!" Because of the suffering of Jewish people through the crusades, their expulsions from the nations of western Europe, particularly Spain, many turned to the emphasis on Messiah, son of David, and the soon coming messianic kingdom. A new center was formed in Tsfat (Safed) in the land of Israel which became a hotbed of messianism as people waited for the Messiah. But this movement lost its influence when Shabbetai Zevi supposedly became a Muslim in 1666, and the Traditional centers in Eastern Europe went back in earnest to an overall study of Talmud. While the rabbis held to the older understanding of a Messiah, son of David, the emphasis was concentrated on pious living and patiently bearing the yoke of the exile.

The Enlightenment and the Messiah

The late 1700's and early 1800's saw some relaxation of attitudes and laws against the Jewish people. In France, after the revolution, many began to taste the freedoms offered them. In the process of entering into the fullness of life there, they set aside some of the more nationalistic aspects of their beliefs, for example, a belief in a Messiah who comes to a state of Israel in the Middle East where the nations will be subject to him. While some Jewish people did not go along, eventually many did, and thus the process of assimilation set in as the means by which Jewish people could be French and also Jews, freely participating in the process of national life. That meant, however, giving up basic messianic distinctives.

A similar movement occurred in Germany with Moses Mendelssohn in the late 1700's. He never intended to begin a new religious expression, but rather labored for civil and religious emancipation; thus an Enlightenment. He opened schools for young people, who flocked to them.

One of Mendelssohn's disciples was David Friedlander (1756–1834), who became the originator of the Reform Movement in Judaism. He urged the removal of all practices and beliefs which had a national coloring. Other leaders followed who hastened, more or less, this new movement and obviously, a belief in the Messiah or messianic kingdom was set aside altogether.

With the major center of Reform Judaism in the United States by the end of the 1800's, two conferences were held to define beliefs, one in Pittsburgh in 1885 and the other in Columbus in 1937. The former created a split in the movement when the decisions simply went too far. One major reason was the desire by the more Reform group to drop any tie to nationalism altogether, which again meant the negation of any belief in a Messiah who is personal. Also, participants wondered what "messianic" kingdom will be brought about by good people, all working together, as the 1885 conference declared: "We extend the hand of fellowship to all who cooperate with us in the establishment of the reign of truth and righteousness among men."

Right after the 1885 conference, another movement began, the Conservative movement, which is really an import from Germany of Zechariah Frankl's formulation when he broke away from the more Reform movement. The Conservative movement is by no means a place where everyone agrees on belief and practice, but one can say that the Traditional and the more conservative of Conservative Jews hold to the same beliefs, particularly to the older version of a Messiah who is personal and the belief in a kingdom brought in by King Messiah. Possibly, the Conservative movement could see modern Israel as a precursor to what will yet happen when the Messiah will come and establish the kingdom.

The presence of the Hasidim, going back to the days of Israel ben Eliezer (known as the Baal Shem Tov, Master of the Good Name, or, the Besht [1700–1760]), has been a significant force within Traditional Judaism to this day. With their emphasis on the attachment to or communion with God, they had great appeal among their co-religionists to enjoy a closer walk with God and thereby draw Redemption near.

A belief in Messiah is very much present, based on an experience of the Baal Shem Tov when he had a vision of the heavenlies. Raphael Patai refers to this in his book, *The Messiah Texts*:

> I entered the Hall of the Messiah where the Messiah was studying Tora with all the Tannaites and the righteous.... And there I saw a very great rejoicing.... And I asked the mouth of the Messiah: "When will the Master come?" And he answered me: "This is how you know: when your teaching will spread and be revealed in the world...what I have taught you and what you have understood, so that they too will be able to make unifications and ascents like you..."

Many among the Hasidim are imbibed with this teaching and they see as one of their many functions to reach out to their fellow Jews, bring them close to the Holy One, and help them realize that God's plan is to one day send the Messiah, even as he told the Besht that the time will come when "...the husks will perish, and that will be the time of grace and salvation."

Signal for a Return to a Messiah Belief?

The Enlightenment movement in the modern period did much to diminish or even dismiss the Messiah emphasis among modernized Jews. But where are we in today's world? Most Jewish people still do not consider the Scriptures as authoritative, much less the traditions, and as a result do not believe in a Messiah who is personal. But there appears to be a growing interest among many Jewish people in the sources of our heritage, and that means an increasing interest in the Messiah and his coming.

In particular, this is true among Jewish people who have recognized Yeshua as the Messiah. More Jewish people have come to faith in Yeshua in this century than in any other, with the exception of the first.

And what is the testimony of these growing numbers of Messianic Jews? Yeshua is the Messiah, who is both human and divine. We have read Matthew's claims in the New Covenant that Yeshua has indeed demonstrated how he can be this mystery person. He is the one, of whom Moses and all the prophets testified, that has come to be our sin bearer, has died for our redemption which we appropriate when we believe in him, was raised from the dead, and is coming again as the powerful son of David who alone can institute the kingdom of peace.

Yeshua alone is the one and only one who can give peace to the heart and soul, rest to weary bodies and aching spirits, a new life that can enable us to live victoriously over our difficulties, and finally, hope so that we are assured of our destination in the world to come, in his presence in the Kingdom of peace.

In *The Messiah Texts,* Raphael Patai refers to a question asked by Hayim Bialik, one of the greatest Hebrew poets of modern times:

> Can one hear the braying of the ass?
> And the child from the cradle raises its head,
> And the mouse peeps out of its hole:
> Is the Messiah coming yet?
> Is the bell of the she-ass ringing?
> And the servant-girl blows into the fire under the kettle,
> And turns her sooty face toward the door:
> Is the Messiah coming yet?
> Can one hear the blast of his trumpet?

Yes, he has indeed come the first time, and we await his coming, with the sound of the loud command, the voice of the archangel, and the trumpet call to join him, when he will come to earth to initiate his kingdom.

10

The Habad Movement and Its Messiah

Carol Calise

The Habad base their concept of the Messiah and the messianic age upon the teachings of the founder, Rabbi Schneur Zalman, and the early Hasidic movement. One of the earlier teachings of Hasidism that affect Habad's view of the messianic age stated that God was literally present in everything. Others in the Jewish community strongly opposed and criticized this doctrine of immanence because they felt God could not and would not exist in the low and earthly things. Habad based their doctrine of divinity on an acosmic concept. According to this teaching, God is the only reality. The universe does not exist distinct from God himself. You cannot accept things on the basis of your senses because such things are an illusion and often misleading. One essence — the divine — fills all things that exist. The Habad are very literal in their belief of the statement "there is nothing that exists beside

Him," as Rachel Elior observes in her book *The Paradoxical Ascent to God.*

The Cosmic Myth

One of the kabbalistic teachings that most influenced Habad Hasidim was the Lurianic Kabbalah. Rabbi Zalman adapted one concept known as the cosmic myth. This myth described the creation of the world as taking place when God contracted part of himself from space. The second phase of this creative process was the emanating of divine lights into vessels. The vessels, however, could not hold the light. There were two potentially opposed powers in the Divine. One of these powers did not cooperate and caused a breaking of the vessels. This evil power imprisoned the divine sparks that were not able to escape to the heavenlies. Thus evil was able to sustain itself off of these trapped divine lights and occupied the lower realm. This theory made evil to be a part of God. The Divine then sent forth another group of emanations, but they were unable to take their rightful position because of these evil powers. The concept of *tikkun* — "mending the broken" or "restoration" — was the answer to this. It became the responsibility of every Jew to do his or her part in this restoration.

The Hasidim made modifications to this theory. First, there was no power struggle that caused the going forth of the divine sparks. Rather, it happened because of God's love for His creation. God intentionally diminished the power of his light because it could not be endured at full capacity. They retained the Lurian concept of trapped sparks, but rejected its concept of evil. Hasidism did not view evil as a part of God but as a *"temporary manifestation of an aspect of divine light."* It would be redeemed and transformed, not destroyed as taught by the Lurian kabbalists. This redemption *(tikkun)* was the responsibility of each Jew. These early teachings are the basis of the modern Habad messianism.

The modern Habad Hasidim believe it is the responsibility of each Jew to prepare the world for the coming of the Messiah by the study of Torah and the observance of its *mitzvot.* Like their early teachers, the modern Habad movement also believes in the divine sparks that are hidden in everything. The study of Torah and the practice of *mitzvot* remove the "outer garment" the world is wearing which hides God's existence, as Shmuel Boteach states it in *The Wolf Shall Lie With the Lamb*. The earth was created to be a place where God could dwell. Man must remove the veil over the earth, thus preparing it to be the dwelling place of God and ushering in the messianic era. All our earthly activities are means to find God, who dwells in and is part of our world. This sets the stage for the appearance of the Messiah and the completion of the process started by man's observance of Torah and *mitzvot*. During the messianic age all the deeds that have been performed throughout the centuries will come together and dispel the darkness that veils the Godly essence of this world. At his coming, the Messiah will dispel the final traces of darkness, so that God will openly dwell on the earth.

Two Views Reconciled

The Habad base many of their concepts concerning the Messiah on the writings of Maimonides (1135–1204). Maimonides stated that the Messiah would be mortal, a great prophet, and active in Torah study, observing the *mitzvot* of the Torah like King David, urging all Israel to observe Torah, fighting the wars of God, removing all obstacles in the world to Torah observance, and would rebuild the Temple and gather in the dispersed among the nations. The purpose of the Messiah performing these functions is to enable all Jews to observe the Torah and practice its *mitzvot* perfectly. Maimonides emphasized the natural order of things and resisted any supernatural or miraculous idea of the Messiah.

Another scholar who influenced the Habad concept of Messiah was Nachmanides (1194–1270). He stood in opposition to Maimonides' rejection of the supernatural and miraculous aspects of the Messiah. Nachmanides opposed Maimonides allegorical approach to messianic prophecies and took a literal interpretation of many of them.

Rabbi Schneerson reconciled the two views of these scholars and based his argument on this quotation from the Talmud:

> It is written: "Behold one like a son of man came on the clouds of heaven" (Daniel 7:13); however, it is also written, "Your king will come like a poor man riding on a donkey" (Zechariah 9:9). If the Jewish people are found worthy of the redemption, then the Messiah will come "on the clouds of heaven"; if they do not merit, he will come "like a poor man riding on a donkey" (*Sanhedrin* 98a).

Rabbi Schneerson stated two possibilities for how the Messiah will come. He will come with miracles if the Jewish people are living a life of excellence. If the Jewish people are lax in this area, the Messiah will come in an ordinary manner. This places the burden on the righteousness of the Jewish people to prepare the world for a miraculous Messiah.

A Messiah in Each Generation

There is the belief in Judaism that within each generation there is one who has the potential to be the Messiah. The Habad believed that Rabbi Schneerson was the Messiah. He fulfilled the qualifications given by Maimonides and messianic prophecies. Rabbi Schneerson himself said nothing publicly to encourage or discourage his followers to hold this belief. He told his followers in recent years that they were now in the final stages of redemption, the *tikkun* (mending of the world) taught in the early history of the movement.

Even with his illness, they still maintained that he was the Messiah. Many outsiders questioned the issue of a successor for Rabbi Schneerson. The response most often given was that there is no need to worry about that because the Messiah will come.

Jack Shamash stated, "Our Rebbe embodies the messianic ideal. We talk openly about him being the Messiah, and we are sure we will see the Messiah before the end of the Rabbi's days."

Craig Horowitz reported in an article written for *New York*

Magazine, "They have no doubt that he is the redeemer that Jews have been praying for and anticipating for thousands of years."

In February 1994 a special meeting was held at Habad headquarters. It was led by Rabbi Shmuel Butman, who is the leader of the Messiah campaign of Habad. In the meeting he stated, "This is the last generation of those of exile and the first generation of redemption." When the crowd finished a prayer, Butman looked up toward the ceiling and implored God to "hear us and give the rebbe a sign to reveal himself." The men began to sing wildly: "Long live our master, our teacher, and our rebbe, King Moshiach forever."

His followers were believing and praying for a miraculous recovery. After his stroke in March 1994 they placed ads proclaiming him to be Messiah. One ad in the *Manhattan Jewish Sentinel* (20–24 April 1994) entitled "How Can the Rebbe Be Moshiach, If He is Ill?" applied Isaiah 53 as an explanation to Schneerson's sufferings. They felt that his death would not invalidate his messiahship. It is this aspect of their messianism that most attracts opposition from mainstream Judaism.

A Messiah at the Forefront Again

Rabbinic Judaism's concept of the Messiah and a messianic age contains historical and ethnic-national redemptive elements. Even with the addition of spiritual and eschatological elements, the historical aspect remained central to its messianism. The messianic idea became a part of tradition because it was an abstract idea. At the moment it became more than that, conflict came between it and the tradition of which it was now a part. The rabbis have rejected messianic movements throughout the years because of fear. They moved messianism "into the realm of pure faith and inaction, leaving the redemption to God alone and not requiring the activity of men" as Gershom Scholem has formulated it in *The Messianic Idea of Judaism.*

The Habad's messianism has brought this issue to the forefront of Jewish thought and life once again. Most feel Schneerson was not the Messiah and are against promoting the concept of

Messiah as you would some product you are trying to sell. There is fear that this proclamation will bring disaster to the Jewish people. In 1992 Arthur Hertzberg, who was vice-president of the World Jewish Congress, wrote that Jews could not believe in the imminent appearance of the Messiah. He feels that the messianic fervor is a danger and that Jews should worry about "cultivating decency" and let God worry about redeeming the world in his time.

The literary editor of *The New Republic*, Leon Wieseltier said, according to Lucelle Lagnado, "The Lubavitcher's messianic activism is probably the greatest outrage against Jewish tradition. It goes against not only a vast tradition of Jewish theology." This statement clearly illustrates the tension and conflict that arises between any concrete messianic ideology and the tradition that it is a part of. Yet, because Habad is an international movement and so aggressive in its proselytizing efforts, it has affected the vast majority of Judaism in a unique way. For years the Messiah issue has been a neglected doctrine of Judaism. Now it is being brought out of the abstract realm and is challenging the Jewish community to deal with the concrete reality of a Messiah.

11

Renewed Interest in Messianic Texts

Tsvi Sadan

Rabbi Menachem Mendel Schneerson of Lubavitch was not unique in his role as a would-be Messiah. He was but the latest of a long list of messiahs who came to save the Jewish nation. From Judah the Galilean and Theudas through Bar Kokhba, and Asher Lammlein, time and again messianic figures have both nourished and shattered the messianic hope of Israel. At times, the disappointment and despair created by these pseudo-messiahs was so great that mass conversions of Jewish people took place. (This occured in 1502 when Lammlein, the expected Messiah failed to fulfill his role. For more about this event, see Abba Hillel Silver, *A History of Messianic Speculation in Israel*). The Habad movement is the contemporary manifestation of the continual Jewish hope for the Messiah. The death of their Rebbe revealed once again the inadequacy of the prevailing Jewish understanding of the identity of the Messiah.

According to Habad scholars, the hope that the Messiah will manifest himself as a great rabbi is based on the Oral Torah, the Talmud. Since much of Habad's understanding about the Messiah depends on the interpretation of one Talmudic text, it is worth quoting parts from this passage:

> Rabbi Johanan said: [the world was created only] for the sake of the Messiah: What is his [the Messiah's] name? — The School of Rabbi Shila said: His name is Shiloh, for it is written, until Shiloh come (Genesis 49:10). The School of Rabbi Yannai said: His name is Yinnon, for it is written, His name shall endure for ever: e'er the sun was, his name is Yinnon (Psalm 72:17).... Rabbi Nahman said: If he [the Messiah] is of those living [today], it might be one like myself, as it is written, And their nobles shall be of themselves, and their governors shall proceed from the midst of them (Jeremiah 30:21, The Babylonian Talmud, *Sanhedrin* 98b).

This passage was taken to mean that the disciples of Rabbi Shila and Rabbi Yannai each saw their master as the potential Messiah and Rabbi Nahman even ascribed this potentiality to himself. In addition, Jewish identification of the Messiah greatly relied upon the example set by Rabbi Akiva concerning Ben Koziba (or Bar Kokhba who was the leader of the Jewish revolt of 132–135AD), on the assumption that whatever Rabbi Akiva said was a rabbinic ruling for his time and for future generations. Therefore, if Rabbi Akiva was wrong, much of the Jewish teaching about the Messiah cannot stand. The Habad movement accordingly denies any possibility of mistake on the part of Rabbi Akiva. Rabbi Shalom Dov Wolpo, the author of *Long Live King Messiah*, thus writes: "How can anybody possibly say that Rabbi Akiva and the sages of his generation erred in their practical ruling, may God save us, for behold Maimonides learns from them how the ruling for generations should be made." Though by and large the ruling concerning the authority of Rabbi Akiva is agreed upon in Rabbinic Judaism, there have been voices in past times, as well as today, who dare to say that Rabbi Akiva was wrong in declaring Bar Kokhba as Messiah. The disagreement over Rabbi Akiva's teaching was not invented by those who oppose Habad or seek to destroy Judaism. The Palestinian Talmud records two declarations which state that Rabbi Akiva was wrong and that Bar Kokhba was the cause for the destruction brought upon Judea.

Concerning Rabbi Akiva it was said:

Rabbi Shimon son of Yochi said: Rabbi Akiva taught: A star will come out of Jacob [meaning] Koziba will come out of Jacob. When Rabbi Akiva saw Ben Koziba he said: [I] rule that he [Ben Koziba] is the king Messiah. Rabbi Johanan son of Tortah said: Akiva, grass will grow out of your cheeks [you will die] and still the Son of David will not come... (The Jerusalem Talmud, *Taanit* 21a; my translation).

Concerning Bar Kokhba it was said:

Woe to the worthless shepherd, who deserts the flock! May the sword strike his arm and his right eye! May his arm be completely withered, his right eye totally blinded [Zec. 11:17]. You [Koziba] killed Rabbi Elazar from Modi'in [who was] the Arm of Israel.... Immediately [after this proclamation] Bethar was captured and Ben Koziba was killed. (The Jerusalem Talmud, *Taanit* 21a; my translation; see also The Babylonian Talmud, *Sanhedrin* 93b)

In our understanding, Habad is wrong in attributing infallibility to Rabbi Akiva and Maimonides, but that does not mean to say that everything these two great sages said and did was false. At the very least, one can say that it was Maimonides who kept the messianic hope alive. It was he who rekindled the hope for the coming of the Messiah as a part of the Jewish faith at a time when many Jews were losing sight for their coming redemption. In much the same way, it is the Habad movement which is largely responsible for renewing the messianic hope in the Jewish heart today. In its feverish excitement over the Messiah, Habad turns the attention of many to reconsider traditional Jewish interpretation of biblical texts which speak about the Messiah, his role, image, and the time of his arrival. Habad, in the words of Joseph Klausner, puts back on the Jewish agenda the suggestion that "indeed, the messianic idea is possibly the brightest of all the precious stones in the adorned crown of Judaism."

In its attempt to prove that Rabbi Menachem Mendel Schneerson was the potential Messiah, Habad has used biblical texts and messianic ideas that up until a few decades ago were not even whispered in hiding places. For example, an idea like the pre-existence of King Messiah was understood from Genesis 1:2, "The Spirit of God was hovering over the waters" (this understanding comes from the Aramaic translation of the Bible). Another example is Habad's attempt to prove that the Messiah should be a priest, king and a prophet all at the same time. To do it Habad used Isaiah 52:13 "see, my servant will act wisely; he will be raised and lifted up and highly exalted." Accordingly, the Messiah will be *lifted up* from Moses, and Moses is seen as a priest, king and prophet (see *Yalkut Shimoni* on this verse). Habad also sees the Messiah as the one who brings a new law, an idea that is based on Isaiah 51:4, "The Law will go out from me." The sages taught on this verse that "a new law will go out from me" (see *Yalkut Shimoni* on this verse). These are only but a few examples of Habad's teaching which may surprise those who have been trained to think that such concepts are exclusively "Christian." In the following brief review, we will closely follow Habad's unique interpretation of two biblical verses.

Maybe the most significant of all is the renewed interest in Isaiah 53. Ever since Rashi (11th century) introduced his interpretation that the suffering servant is Israel, the messianic message of this chapter has practically been abandoned within Jewish circles. Habad, however, has brought back forgotten attributes of the Messiah based on this chapter.

On the verse "a man of sorrow, and familiar with suffering"(Isaiah 53:3), Menachem Brod, author of *The Age of the Messiah: Redemption and the Coming of the Messiah in Jewish Sources*, writes the following:

> That in the beginning people despised and ridiculed him, but in the end he is revealed as someone who supersedes everybody. Many interpreters think that this image refers to the nation of Israel, which in the time of exile suffered much and was at her lowest point, but in the time of redemption she is exalted and lifted up above all nations. But there are interpreters who interpret this chapter as referring to the Messiah.

Rabbi Wolpo, after bringing extensive proof from different Jewish sources that the Messiah, not Israel, is the suffering servant, goes on to say:

> And behold ever since his esteemed holiness, our lord, teacher and Rabbi, may he live a long and good life, amen, ascended to the prince's throne, the ordeal of his suffering did not stop. Out of extensive fasting he was afflicted, like our holy Rabbi, with terrible suffering of his teeth, so that already from a young age, not even a single tooth was left in his mouth. And in 1977 he went through terrible suffering in his pure heart, and even now, already for a few months, he suffers greatly because of our many transgressions.

Although trivializing the suffering of the Messiah to toothache, Habad has nevertheless grasped the idea that the Messiah is to suffer because of man's sin. This admission is remarkable, considering the fact that for generations believers in Yeshua were bitterly ridiculed by those who insisted that the scriptures never taught us Jews to believe in man as a sacrifice. In a strange and unexpected way, Habad is now reclaiming this forbidden chapter for the Messiah. Once an alien and repulsive concept, it has become one of the foundations of Habad's messianic theology. At last, some Jews are beginning to understand that one of the Messiah's purposes is to atone for man's sin.

Another verse that receives a new treatment at Habad's hand is Genesis 49:10: "The scepter will not depart from Judah, nor the ruler's staff from between his feet." Though it never lost its messianic meaning, this verse was used to justify Menachem Mendel Schneerson's genealogy. Since genealogy is one of the most important elements of any teaching about the Messiah, the Rebbe's genealogy presents a potential problem. According to Habad, he was from the house of David not only through his father but also through his mother.

Habad, aware of the difficulties presented by maternal lineage, finds an interesting solution to this problem. A passage in the Talmud explains that the word scepter refers to the Jewish leader of the diaspora and the term ruler's staff refers to the head of the Sanhedrin in the land of Israel. The Talmud also records that two great Jewish figures who were heads of the Sanhedrin, Rabbi Yehuda Ha-Nasi, and Rabbi Hillel were from the house of David according to their mothers' lineage (The Jerusalem Talmud, *Kilayim* 9:3). Therefore, the Talmud concludes: "the leader of the diaspora came from the males of David and the head of the Sanhedrin came from the females of David" (ibid.). Habad explains that since the scepter and the ruler's staff have been merged into one person, their Rabbi perfectly fulfills the messianic requirement that the Messiah should come from David according to his paternal and maternal lineage.

Once again we find that despite exaggerated logical gymnastics, Habad is able to admit that the Messiah's Davidic lineage is both paternal and maternal. If we remember the prevalent Jewish contempt for the genealogies recorded in the New Testament, the new way in which Habad sees Messiah's genealogies should not be underestimated.

Can any good thing therefore come out of Crown Heights? Let no one be fooled. The Rebbe was never meant to be, and never will be the Messiah (some Habad people are now saying that Schneerson will be resurrected from the dead to be revealed once and for all as Israel's Messiah). Furthermore, regardless of how close some of Habad's teaching are to the claims of Yeshua's disciples, their antipathy towards them and Yeshua will remain. Nevertheless, in their desire for the Messiah, Habad has unwittingly come closer to the teaching of the New Testament than traditional Jewish thought has ever done before. No one should rejoice when another Messiah passes away, shattering the hope of thousands once again. Rather, with compassionate prayer, those who already know the true Messiah should look forward to the day when Habad will also receive Him, even according to their own teaching.

12

On Calculating the Time of the Messiah's Appearance

Ray Pritz

He was tall with grey hair, well-spoken, with a sophisticated look about him. But he had a very peculiar calling card. On the front, in addition to the normal information, were the words "Do you believe in Jesus? If so, I will see you on April 23, 1981." And on the back of the card: "If not, you will see John F. Kennedy (the Antichrist)." He and his wife moved about Jerusalem during the winter of 1980–81, explaining their eschatology and giving out calling cards. They stayed until their visa expired sometime in June. The End had not come, the Messiah had not appeared, nor had John Kennedy. Even after 23 April they were not ready to admit that perhaps they had been wrong. It would still happen soon, was already happening but only the truly spiritual could discern it.

The Desire to Know the Future

The desire to know the future seems to be universal. When it is combined with religious belief in a critical event which is sure to come on the basis of revealed Scripture, the end result is often the calculation of the time when the event will occur. Several assumptions underlie calculations. The first is that God rules over history and that he knows the exact course and timing of coming events. It is further assumed that God has placed enough information in the Bible to make it possible to figure out when the expected events will occur. It should only be necessary to apply the right tools to the right scriptures to discover when it will all take place.

While the man in the above example was a Christian, calculations of the coming of the Messiah have been at least as frequent in Judaism as in Christianity. In the 20 centuries of the Common Era literally hundreds of dates have been suggested by rabbis and other Jewish thinkers. The most comprehensive study of this phenomenon was done earlier this century by the well-known American scholar, the late Rabbi Abba Hillel Silver, in his book *A History of Messianic Speculation in Israel* (1927).

Silver limited himself to the period between the destruction of the Second Temple and the end of the 17th century, although for the second edition in 1959 he added a brief overview of Jewish messianic expectations since the time of Shabbetai Zevi. For each of the seven periods into which he divides the 16 centuries covered, he describes the political and spiritual background of the period, citing factors which influenced those who tried to calculate the end. After an analysis of the calculations made, he adds to each section a brief history of the messianic pretenders who appeared during the same period.

I do not intend to review Silver's book. Rather, I would like to use it to help discern patterns which tend to characterize messianic speculation. Is the messianic fervor in the Habad movement in our times something out of the ordinary, or is it something one might have expected, a phenomenon the outcome of which might even be predicted?

The Frequency and Popularity of Speculating

One is first impressed by the sheer numbers of calculations made. With the notable exception of the 15th century, when disappointment was great after highly popular dates passed with no Messiah, there was hardly a generation without at least one learned man ready to predict the date of Messiah's appearance. Many made more than one prediction or designated a period during which the Messiah would come, rather than naming a specific year. Some even predicted one year and, when it had passed uneventfully, adjusted their figures and tried again.

Starting from a Critical Event

To calculate a target date, one needs to start from somewhere. Presumably the starting date will coincide with a significant event, and the rabbis kept a few of these very busy serving as springboards. The most popular was the destruction of the Second Temple, which popular chronology dated in 68CE. The very earliest of these was a tradition which said that the Messiah was born on the day the Temple was destroyed. This would have placed his appearance and redeeming activity in the early part of the Second Century, a fact which may have helped fuel the Bar Kokhba revolt. The disappointment which followed that revolt caused the rabbis to discourage such calculation (and specifically the reading of the book of Daniel). When further calculations were made, they took the idea that the present exile would be of the same length as the exile in Egypt, around 400 years. This pushed the expected date into the safer distant future, somewhere in the fifth century.

After the rise of Islam, the date of the *hejira* (622) was frequently employed by Jewish writers, many of whom saw in the Moslems the potential deliverers from the hand of Rome (Silver, 36f). In later centuries the fall of Constantinople to the Turks in 1453 would figure in the speculations. This event was also used by Martin Luther as a starting point when he arrived at 1558 as the date for the eschaton (*Table Talks,* no. 427). By way of example, Isaac Abrabanel, in his *Wells of Salvation* (1496), interprets Daniel 12 to indicate the fall of Edom in 1453 followed 50 years later (the amount of time from the start of the Babylonian exile until Cyrus gave the Jews permission to return to Jerusalem) by the final redemption in 1503. Other popular historical turning points were the destruction of the First Temple and the fall of Rome.

The Use of Biblical Ideas and Texts

One of the most common features of messianic calculation is the use of a few statements of Scripture which seem to be intended for that very purpose. These come mostly from the book of Daniel:

1) time, times and half a time (7:25; 12:7).
2) 2300 mornings and evenings (8:14).
3) 70 weeks, including 7 weeks, 62 weeks and one week (9:24–27).
4) 1290 days (12:11).
5) 1335 days (12:12).

By varying the starting points or combining with other scriptures, dozens upon dozens of different dates are arrived at using the same few verses.

The biblical exiles of Israel from its land were seen as precursors of the present exile. Just as they had lasted x number of years, so also would this exile be limited to the same amount of time ("The final redemption will be like the first redemption," *Numbers Rabbah* 11:3). The picture was somewhat complicated by the fact that the Bible gives different lengths of time for the exiles. So, for example, the Babylonian exile lasted 70 years but could also be said to have been 52 years long. Similarly, the exile in Egypt is variously given as 210, 400 or 430 years. This "complication" had a hidden blessing, because it provided the speculators with greater flexibility. Bahja ben Asher (d. 1340) wrote in 1291 that the present exile has three possible ending dates. Using 68CE as his base, he said the redemption should have come in

1218 if Israel had been worthy. The next date would be 1358, and, failing that, the latest possible date would be 1403.

The biblical 50 year Jubilee cycle also provided potential calculating material. If the Jubilee was the time of release from debts and slavery and especially the return of land to its original owners (Leviticus 25), then surely it must figure somehow in God's grand plan of redemption and the restoration of the land of Israel to the people of Israel. Thus, for example, early speculations centered on the 85th Jubilee, which would fall between 440 and 490. Rabbi Judah (3rd century) is said to have had a revelation from Elijah: "The world will endure no less than 85 Jubilees, and in the last Jubilee the son of David will come" (The Babylonian Talmud, *Sanhedrin* 97b). Rav Ashi, who lived in the early fifth century, tempered the calculation with "Before the 85th Jubilee you need not expect him at all. After the 85th Jubilee you may expect him." Similarly, the 19-year cycles (intimated but not expressly stated in Scripture) provided a basis for calculation.

Gematria and Astrology

It was not a great step from the concept that the Bible text was holy to the idea that the words, indeed the letters themselves, were divine. If this was so, then deeper meaning might be hidden even in the numerical value of the letters of particular words and phrases. This is the basic assumption of rabbinic use of gematria. God has carefully chosen the words of holy writ so that they communicate meaning not only literally but also numerically. So, for example, when Jacob tells his sons to go down to Egypt, the word for "go down" in Hebrew has three letters with the numerical value of 210, which is the number of years the rabbis said (on other grounds) that the Israelites were actually in Egypt (cf. Rashi — 11th century — for the full calculation).

With all of the biblical injunctions against worship of heavenly bodies, it is surprising to find religious Jews turning to astrology for an answer to the riddle of the date of redemption. Silver shows that Jewish belief in stellar and planetary influence on men's lives was common throughout the history of Israel. The use of astrological divination to calculate the Messiah's appearance did not begin, however, until the 11th century with Solomon ibn Gabirol. The primary influence at the time was the resurgence of astrology during the Arabic renaissance.

The End is Near

The reader will have noticed in several of the examples given above the closeness of the dates calculated to the lifetime of the one doing the calculation. While Silver does not dwell on this phenomenon, it stands out to the reader of his book. Time and again the speculators seem to arrive at dates within their own foreseeable lifetime. Does this say something about human nature and the psychology behind the desire to figure out the time of the end? Victor Hugo's dictum "apres moi le deluge" may sum up how most people see the "end time": somehow when I go that will be the end of everything.

SAADIA GAON (882–942), who tried to harmonize the various figures given in Daniel, seems to have expected the redemption in the year 968, a popular date elsewhere which gave rise to some messianic excitement.

JUDAH HALEVI (1080–1141) used the rise of Mohammed as his base, added 500 years, and arrived at a date around 1130. Earlier calculations had used the more natural figure of 400 years, coinciding with the exile in Egypt, but when the year 1022 passed, an extra hundred years was added.

ABRAHAM BAR HIYYA went through an elaborate set of calculations and arrived at several dates, the first of which was 1136, the very year of his death.

MAIMONIDES (1135–1204), who wrote a strongly worded letter discouraging the futile exercise of calculating the end, could not, even so, forebear the temptation to relate an old family tradition which predicted the Messiah's appearance in 1216.

LEVI BEN GERSHON (Gersonides, 1288–1344), like so many others, based his speculation on an analysis of Daniel 12 and arrived at a date within his own foreseeable lifetime. Silver writes:

Gersonides maintains that there is clear reference to Rome, to the final Dispersion, and to the final Redemption in the closing chapter of Daniel. The definite date is given in chapter 12, verse 11. Twelve hundred and ninety years will elapse from the destruction to the Redemption; the destruction was in the year 3828AM [since the creation]; the Redemption will therefore be in the year 5118AM = 1358CE The figure given in the following verse, 1335, which is 45 years later, refers to the end of the Messianic wars against Gog and Magog.

"The calculation is quite simple," says Gersonides. "The reason why previous calculators went astray was due to the fact that each one tried to bring the Messianic date as close to his own time as possible."

Conclusion

Those who tell us today that the messianic age is about to dawn are in good company. We have good verses from Daniel which can be put to service to prove it; we are within a generation or so of a critical event, the rebirth of the Jewish state; we are approaching the year 2000 (round numbers have also always been popular); and we naturally tend to sense that it must happen in our lifetime. The hope for redemption is strong in us, some would even say that God placed it there. Certainly it can be a positive and healthy motivation. But when will the Redeemer actually appear?

The times and occasions are set by my Father's own authority, and it is not for you to know when they will be. But...you will be witnesses for me in Jerusalem, in all of Judea and Samaria, and to the ends of the earth (Jesus of Nazareth, Acts 1:7–8).

13

Jewish Objections to Jesus

Arnold Fruchtenbaum

Jesus is all too often judged by 20th century Judaism rather than first-century or biblical Judaism. The question, however, can never be, "Is Jesus the Messiah in accordance with Judaism today?" Judaism today is too fragmented, with messianic views ranging from "He will come" to "What Messiah! There will be no Messiah." The fact is that most Jews today do not believe in any Messiah at all. The real issue is, "Is Jesus the Messiah of Old Testament Judaism?"

Today's Judaism is different from the Judaism of the Old Testament or even the Judaism of Jesus' day. Modern Judaism is certainly not the "father of Christianity." At best it is its brother, with biblical Judaism being the father of both. If one were to read the books of the Old Testament and compare their teachings with the Judaism of today, one could almost conclude that modern Judaism is a completely new religion! Certainly there are similarities between Judaism then and now. Yet similarities exist between various religions and they are, nevertheless, distinct one from another. The real issue is whether Jesus is the Messiah of the Old Testament. The messiahship of Jesus must stand or fall on no other criterion than his fulfillment of the messianic prophecies of the Scriptures.

What Kind of God Do You Have?

Some Jewish objections to the messiahship of Jesus rest on questioning the virgin birth and Jesus' resurrection from the dead. Objections to these two matters are, however, not the real issue in themselves. The real issue is what kind of God one believes in. The question is not, "Is such a thing as the virgin birth possible?" Or, "Is such a thing as resurrection from death possible?" From the strictly human viewpoint they are not. The real question is, "Can God do such things?" If he cannot, he is not much of a God. But if God is God, and all that this particular title infers, includes, and indicates, he can do anything he wants to do. The only possible limits to God are the limits he places on himself.

If God is all powerful, things like the virgin birth and the resurrection are easy things for him to accomplish. It is an amazing inconsistency to allow that God had created the heavens and the earth and then to doubt his ability to bring about a virgin birth. If he can create the wonder and vastness of the universe and all the complexity of the single cell, the virgin birth and the resurrection are very simple matters. For a Jew who believes in God, there is no reason to doubt the miracle of the virgin birth. The real question is, "Did it happen with the birth of Jesus?" The Old Testament said that it *would* happen with the Messiah. The New Testament said that it *did* happen with Jesus.

Jesus Didn't Bring Peace, Did He?

The most common objection one hears to the messiahship of Jesus is this: "He could not be the Messiah since he did not bring peace." Well, since he was not accepted, he could not very well bring peace, could he? Furthermore, the purpose of the Messiah's first coming, or as the early rabbis would have it, the purpose of the coming of the first Messiah, the Messiah, the Son of Joseph, was not to bring peace but to suffer and die. Peace would come through the coming of the second Messiah, the Messiah, the Son of David, or as the New Testament would have it, by the second coming of the Messiah. So the messiahship of Jesus must first be judged on whether he did suffer and die for sin, and then on whether those who believed in him received their justification and forgiveness of sins. That he suffered and died for the sins of Israel is the testimony of the eyewitness accounts we have in the New Testament. That Jews have been receiving and experiencing the forgiveness of their sins through faith in the substitutionary death of Jesus has been testified by many. Talmudic Judaism and the New Testament agree that there would be one coming of a Messiah to suffer and die, which would precede the coming of the Messiah to bring peace. The point of difference is the former's claim of two different Messiahs, and the latter's claim of one and the same person, Jesus.

While it is true that Jesus did not bring peace, that was not the purpose of Messiah's first coming. This is not a valid argument against his messiahship. For Jesus will yet come again and will yet bring peace.

Messiah and Son of God.

As to the claim of Jesus to be the Son of God, one objection reads like this:

> The New Testament knows Jesus as the Son of God and as Messiah. Judaism, however, does not acknowledge a Son of God who was set apart and elevated above other human beings. The Jewish conviction is that all men are equal before God and no mortal can claim divinity.

Here is an example of how the messiahship of Jesus is judged purely on the basis of modern Judaism. Jesus could not be the Messiah, the writer says, since Judaism does not acknowledge a Son of God to begin with. The writer would have been more honest had he said that Judaism *as he knows it*, which is only modern Judaism, does not acknowledge a Son of God. (In the case of Reform Judaism, there would be no Messiah to begin with.) The writer effectively ignores centuries of Jewish theological treatments that certainly do treat the Messiah as being a Son of God. Had the writer taken the time to look at the early rabbinical interpretations of Psalm 2, it would have led him to avoid such a rash statement, which even Rashi (11th century) did not do. The question is whether Jesus is the Messiah of the Old Testament — not whether he is the Messiah of modern Judaism.

And of course, Jews cannot believe that any man could become God and that is why Jews cannot accept Jesus, say the rabbis. To begin with, the fact that a man cannot become God is very true; no man can claim divinity. This is where modern Judaism has misconstrued the teachings of the New Testament. The New Testament never claimed that Jesus was a man who became God. This is heresy. This goes contrary to Judaism of any form, biblical, rabbinic or otherwise, and it also goes contrary to the Christian faith. Neither the New Testament nor Jesus ever taught that there was a man who became God.

The New Testament claims the reverse: It was God who became a man in the person of Jesus of Nazareth. If God became a man, this man would certainly be superior to other men. He would now be the God-Man. Certainly Judaism does not dare claim that God cannot become a man if he wanted to. The God of biblical Judaism is all powerful. God can do anything he wants to. If there is anything God cannot do, he is less than God. So the real question is, "Did God choose to become a man?" not "Can he?" The claim is that God became a man. It is amazing how so many rabbinic writings about Jesus refuse to discuss this very point and insist on discussing how could a man become God.

Other common objections also miss the real point. One such objection is the fact that Jesus forgave sins, which is something only God can do. Again this is true — only God can forgive sins. But if Jesus is the God-Man, God who became a man, the forgiving of sins would be part of the authority of this God-Man.

The Miracles of Jesus

Another objection of this nature centers around the fact that Jesus performed his miracles in his own name. This objection, as voiced by one Jewish writer, runs as follows:

> The Hebrew prophets too, performed miracles; but they stressed that they did so as God's instruments. When Elijah revived the son of the widow, he did not say that he had wrought that miracle as Jesus did on a similar occasion.

First of all, it might be said that many times Jesus claimed that he was doing his miracles by the power and authority of the Spirit of God. It is true that the prophets did miracles and gave God the credit, but again, Messiah was not going to be just another man or just another prophet. Rabbinic theories taught that the Messiah, because he had the name of God himself, will be able to do things in his own name. That is why the Messiah kept playing such a prominent role in rabbinic theology. That is why the Jewish people throughout the centuries looked forward to the coming of the Jewish Messiah. The Messiah would have such authority and such power that he would be able to accomplish great things in his own name. Jesus claimed to be that Messiah and so should in fact have been able to do those things in his own name. As the author admits, Jesus did accomplish those things in his own name. By doing so in his own name, he substantiates his messiahship rather than disproves it.

The Majority and the Minority

A different kind of objection is raised over and over again: "If Jesus was the Messiah, why don't the rabbis believe in him?" Or it may be stated like this: "If Jesus is the Messiah, how come very few Jews believe this?" The implication here is that something cannot be true for the Jew unless most rabbis or most Jewish people accept it to be true. In other words, the implication is that truth is determined by majority vote.

However, truth is not determined by majority vote. As we look at our sacred history, we will discover over and over again that it was always the minority of Jews who obeyed the revelation of God. The prophets called the small group of believers the remnant of Israel. It was always that remnant of Israel that accepted what God had to say through his prophets. The majority by and large rejected it, including the religious leaders of that day.

But often the objection is raised that it is not logical and it is not Jewish to believe in Jesus. Well, that depends on the issue of who Jesus really is. Now suppose Jesus really is the Messiah. For the sake of argument, let the premise be allowed that he is the Messiah. Surely then the most natural, Jewish thing to do is to believe in him — that is logical enough. If Jesus is the Messiah, it is Jewish to believe in Jesus. And believing in Jesus if he is the Messiah makes a Jewish person not less Jewish but more Jewish. That actually makes him a completed Jew, because he has the relationship that the first Jew had, a relationship with God by faith.

Many objections raised are often fronts for a real objection that is not often voiced: the fear that if one who is Jewish accepts Jesus, he will cease to be a Jew. This is a real Jewish fear. He will cease to be a Jew and become a Gentile. Yet those Jews who do believe in Jesus firmly maintain that Jesus did not destroy their Jewishness.

14

What Kind of Person is Jesus?

Walter Riggans

The great issue between Jews and Christians today, at least in most quarters, is no longer whether or not Jesus was a bona fide Jewish teacher; nor is there any bitter controversy as to whether or not he played a prophetic role in the life of Israel at the end of the Second Temple Period, though some will want to deny him the prophetic mantle. No, attention has been focused elsewhere in our generation.

The Identity of Jesus

Clearly the largest single difference between Jews and Christians on the issue of the identity of Jesus is found in the answer to the question of whether he is not only a great Jewish teacher of his time, and possibly also a prophetic figure of some considerable stature, but also the promised Messiah of Israel. We have come full circle to the opening generations of the Common Era.

The Jewish world as a whole does not accept that Jesus is the Messiah. However, the reason for this has much more to do with the Jewish community's terrible suffering at the hands of the Church than it has to do with any careful and honest assessment of the person, teaching and work of Jesus himself. Having said that, of course, no one could fail to sympathize with the Jewish attitude which says that you can perhaps best judge a person by his or her followers.

On the other hand, Jesus still calls to Jewish people to let him speak to them face to face, as it were. The fact that there is strong pressure from the Jewish community against this should not be allowed to prevent an open attitude to Jesus. In fact several Jewish scholars have already begun to challenge this anti-Jesus pressure. But instead of going any further on this matter, it is necessary to introduce the actual teachings and actions of Jesus, in order to provide clues to what will be found when the Gospels are opened for the Jewish community.

What Kind of Person is Jesus?

What kind of person is Jesus? He is a "people person," as we like to say nowadays. All sorts of people wanted to spend time with him, as we read in the Gospels; and this is just as true today.

In the Gospels we see him in the company of street people (including prostitutes), everyday workers (like fishermen and tradesmen), religious leaders of different persuasions, women of all sorts (whom Jesus gave healing, forgiveness and respect), and political extremists (as the zealots were). People were not always comfortable around him, but his spiritual and moral challenges to people struck home very deeply, attracting those who were sincerely searching for a right relationship with God. It is clear from the Gospels that Jesus had a real concern and respect for women. What is also evident is his love for children, and for the disadvantaged of all types.

Several times we are told of his strong compassion for people in pain and in difficult circumstances. Much of the account preserved for us tells us about his commitment to healing people. Jesus went so far as to heal the sick on the Sabbath. There was great pressure from the religious establishment to postpone until another day any healing which could be put off without danger to the suffering person. But Jesus countered by insisting that there could not be any better day than the Sabbath on which to heal the sick, thus celebrating God's good creation and re-creation of life!

Another characteristic of Jesus about which we are often told is his authority as a teacher, and as a living model, of the life and love of God. This is not to denigrate in any way the wisdom or piety of any others, but it is the recognition that Jesus had (and has) authority which was, quite simply, amazing. Jesus' words had power in two senses. On the one hand people knew that he spoke the truth when he questioned them or answered their questions, whether they liked the truth or not; on the other hand he was able to do everything he said he could do, in terms of healing people and performing miracles.

The Kingdom of Heaven

Central to Jesus' teaching was the reality and the imminence of the Kingdom of God, or, as he would have called it, the Kingdom of Heaven. This is not a geographical term, of course, but means the active rule of God in the world. When God is in charge of your life then you are part of the Kingdom of God. Also characteristic was Jesus' stress on the truth that God is our Father, concerned about us, loving us, longing for a real relationship with us. He spoke to God calling Him "Abba," a term of warm affection, loving respect, and trusting surrender.

Using the texts of Deuteronomy 6:5 (love the Lord your God with all your heart, soul, and strength) and Leviticus 19:18 (love your neighbor as yourself), Jesus taught that life was about loving God with all of one's being, and then also loving every other person whom God had created in his image.

This all adds up to an incredibly attractive and powerful person who made an irreversible difference to all those who came into real contact with him. Jesus was killed on an execution stake by the Roman authorities (though his death was not mourned by certain Jewish leaders). The Gospels then go on to tell us that

God raised him back to life, and that he shared the power of his resurrection with his followers. Countless followers of Jesus from that time till now, numbering many Jewish believers among them, testify that he is as alive today as he ever was. He still makes that real difference to people, Jewish and non-Jewish, who come into real contact with him.

15

The Triune God and the Jew Jesus

Kai Kjær-Hansen

In order to enter the Church of the Nativity in Bethlehem one has to bow down — the entrance door is very low. Therein is beautiful symbolism. The mystery of the incarnation, the fact that Israel's God became man in Jesus of Nazareth, also calls on us to bow down, in faith and adoration. Incarnation and Trinity are connected. It is a matter of who God is and how he reveals himself, and how humans come into fellowship with him. Focus will here be on one of the aspects of the doctrine of the Trinity, namely that the Jew Jesus of Nazareth is the Son of God and therefore, according to traditional Christian belief, divine. Messianic Jews share this belief — with rare exceptions.

The Trinity — Not Polytheism

Christians and Messianic Jews profess their faith in God the Father, God the Son and God the Holy Spirit. For want of a better expression the term "Trinity" is used. The term "Trinity" is *not* found in the Bible. The subject-matter which the doctrine of the Trinity expresses is biblical. Therefore some may well have difficulties with the term while they adhere to the substance. This is the case with Messianic Jews today. The reason is that in a Jewish context the term Trinity can easily be misunderstood, as if Christianity was a religion with three gods. And if the otherwise very different Jewish groupings agree on anything, it is profession of the one God, Israel's God, as expressed in the *Shema*, Israel's "creed": "Hear, O Israel: The Lord our God, the Lord is One" (Deuteronomy 6:4). The observant Jew prays these words twice every day — the less observant Jew does so when in danger or need or the hour of death. God is one! Judaism is monotheistic.

When the God of Israel is called the Triune God, it neither follows that the God of Christianity — the expression is admittedly ugly — becomes the God of Israel to a lesser degree. According to Christian faith, the God of Abraham, Isaac and Jacob is the Father of Jesus the Messiah — and is our Father. He is the only God. And it is Christianity's affirmation that from eternity the God of Israel has been the Triune God. That the God of Israel reveals himself as Father, Son and Holy Spirit is a concept which has been handed down by the first Jesus-believing Jews, not something a much later period's non-Jewish theologians invented. The non-Jewish theologians in the early Church only systematized the concept.

Idolaters and Non-Idolaters

In the Middle Ages Christians were often considered idolaters by Jewish scholars. But at the beginning of the 14th century Rabbi Menachem Ha-Me'iri in Provence, France argued that Christians were not idolaters. This view has now become the dominant one among Jews. A Christian — of non-Jewish descent, mind you — who professes his faith in the Triune God is not an idolater. It is different with a person of Jewish descent. The traditional Jewish attitude is still that Jews who believe in the Triune God are idolaters — even if they refrain from using the term Trinity. For the doctrine of the Trinity may be expressed in other terms, as Jewish scholars have correctly observed.

It is characteristic of the mainstream of Messianic Jews in recent years that they do not use the term Trinity in their statements of faith. It simply feels too un-Jewish. But it does not necessarily imply that the doctrine of the Messiah or the Holy Spirit has been weakened. The point is that they want to use biblical language and biblical categories, not terms found only outside the Bible.

In such statements of faith it is usual to begin with a strong emphasis on the unity of God. Sometimes it is stressed that it is a compound unity, which is a possible reading of the Hebrew word used in the Shema Israel (God is One). This compound unity consists of three persons: Father, Son and Holy Spirit. And the divinity of Jesus is stressed in these formulations, if we keep to the mainstream of contemporary Messianic Judaism.

While Messianic Jews through their statements of faith have clearly shown that they are within the biblical and evangelical framework, it may also be noted that so far there have been practically no systematic attempts to describe the relationship between the three persons. Even if such contributions do not occur concurrently with the growth of the relatively young movement, it would still take theological courage to tell other believers, who stick to biblical terminology and biblical concepts, that they are heretics.

Who Changed God's Diapers?

While theologians — Jewish as well as Christian — generally speak politely and respectfully about each other when they discuss such difficult matters as the Trinity and the divinity of Jesus, the tone is distinctly different with Jewish anti-missionaries who endeavor to warn Jews against faith in Jesus. Here is a sample of how these things are described from an anti-missionary point of view. Shmuel Golding, leader of the Jerusalem Institute of Biblical Polemics, wrote a tract entitled, "Who Changed God's Diapers?" The subtitle reads, "A Refutation to the Virgin Birth Story and The Son of God Theory." It begins in this way:

> To many people the above question sounds blasphemous, but before throwing this tract away in disgust, please know that millions of Christians believe the God of the universe was once a baby boy.
>
> Jews for Jesus and other messianics have been led astray by Christian missionaries and have accepted for themselves a god who not only had his diapers changed but suckled the breasts of a woman, had to learn obedience and was tempted like any earthly mortal.

Of course these words do not represent all Jews' attitude regarding Jesus, but do give an impression of how some Jews speak about Jesus when they try to warn fellow-Jews against him or to de-program Jews who have come to faith in him. The following statement belongs to Samuel Levine, another anti-missionary:

> I have no quarrel with Christian missionaries who try to convert pagans into becoming Christians. That is highly meritorious, because they are transforming an immoral, primitive person into a more moral and spiritual one. However, this is not true when a Jew becomes a Christian.

These words should be seen in the light of these anti-missionaries' conviction that a Jesus-believing Jew has become an idolater when he worships God the Father, God the Son and God the Holy Spirit.

But this is exactly something the first Jesus-believing Jews taught both Jew and gentile in the first century.

16

The Rebirth of
Messianic Judaism

David Sedaca

The second half of the 20th century has witnessed the rise of Messianic Judaism, a movement that has finally found its niche in the religious world. Today, Messianic Judaism is rapidly growing in different parts of the world: Israel, North and South America, Europe, Australia, New Zealand and South Africa. Because of its history and the impact of such a movement in the light of biblical interpretation, it cannot be dismissed as an experiment to be tested or a fad to be tried out. Any conscious analysis of Messianic Judaism has to be performed against its own historical and biblical backdrop.

What Is Messianic Judaism?

Messianic Judaism is the term used to define a form of lifestyle and worship that fully identifies with Jewish customs and traditions while believing that Yeshua (Jesus) of Nazareth is the promised Messiah of the Jewish Scriptures. At the same time, Messianic Judaism holds most emphatically that it is part of the universal body of Messiah, the Church, but claims the right to express itself, both in its daily life and worship style, in a way that agrees with its Jewish heritage. Messianic Jews believe in maintaining a Jewish expression to their faith, therefore they celebrate all biblical holidays (*Pesach* — Passover, *Succot* — Feast of Tabernacles, *Shavuot* — Pentecost, etc.) which the people of Israel were commanded to observe for all generations.

Another characteristic of this movement is its love and support for the nation of Israel. Messianic Jews usually establish congregations for their worship, even though there are many cases in which Messianic Jews remain formally affiliated with traditional churches. These Messianic congregations are fashioned after the early church of the New Testament. Messianic Jewish congregations, sometimes called Messianic Jewish synagogues, have certain characteristics: worship on the Sabbath, Davidic music and dance and many other Jewish rituals consistent with biblical Jewish traditions. It should be noted that, in full agreement with New Testament teachings, membership is open to both Jew and gentile.

The Reappearance of Messianic Judaism

Messianic Judaism of today did not develop in a vacuum. It is the logical consequence of a process that began 2000 years ago, when a young Jewish man began to preach that the messianic hopes proclaimed by the prophets of Israel were fulfilled in him. Most scholars agree that this man, Yeshua, lived a lifestyle consistent with first-century Judaism. From Jewish records and church historians, we know that, even after the first century, when Messianic Jews ceased to be the leaders of the church, there were individual Jews who believed in Jesus. But Messianic Judaism of today is the latest expression of a process that is over 100 years old. The resurgence of this movement can be traced to Great Britain in the early part of the 19th century. At that time thousands of Jewish people had converted to Christianity, but were losing their Jewish identity. By the middle of the 19th century, there were many outstanding Jewish believers in Jesus who began questioning the then prevailing principle that the corollary of accepting Jesus was the forfeiture of one's Jewish heritage. Contacts in England between these Jewish believers ultimately led to the formation of the first body of believers who recognized both their Jewish ancestry and their faith in Jesus as the Messiah of Israel. The name of this association was "Beni Abraham," Children of Abraham.

But it was only with the formation of an umbrella organization that Jewish believers were united in bonds of heritage, witnessing and belief. This organization was the Hebrew Christian Alliance. The idea was first promoted by C. Schwartz of Trinity Chapel, and finally, on 14 May 1867, a resolution was passed to unite all Jewish believers under the umbrella of the Hebrew Christian Alliance and Prayer Union of Great Britain. The organization of this first national alliance led to the establishing of similar alliances in different parts of the world. With the appearance of the first Hebrew Christian Alliance, many Jewish believers in the churches came out into the open declaring their Jewish ancestry. This phenomenon spread like wildfire and, before the turn of the century, there were national alliances of Jewish believers established in many European countries.

Another organization, founded in England in 1883 to unite Jewish believers in prayer support and spiritual bonds, was the Hebrew Christian Prayer Union. The concept was so well received that in less than seven years from its formation its membership rose from 147 to 600, and they established branches in Germany, Norway, Romania, Russia, Israel (then Palestine) and the United States. These national alliances, although closely related with each other, lacked the international structure that would further unite them in their purposes. This need was finally met when, in 1925, all the Hebrew Christian Alliances formed the International Hebrew Christian Alliance (IHCA). Before the outbreak of World War II there were 20 national alliances affiliated with the IHCA. In the words of Hugh Schonfield, an early historian of the modern Messianic movement, "Since 1925, the history of Jewish Christianity becomes in effect the history of the IHCA."

Once Jewish believers tested their strength, they realized that this was just the beginning of a very important movement. Sir Leon Levinson, first president of the IHCA wrote in 1927 in *The Hebrew Christian Quarterly*, the official organ of the IHCA, that the numbers of Jewish believers were roughly distributed as follows: in Vienna, 17,000 accepted Jesus; in Poland, 35,000; in Russia, 60,000; in America and Canada, over 30,000; and in Great Britain, 5000.

The next step forward was to establish a church made up of Jewish believers in which their Jewishness could be emphasized. There had been several successful experiences in this regard. One was the Hebrew Christian movement in Kishinev (in Moldavia, a former Soviet republic) led by Joseph Rabinowitz, a lawyer who founded the first Hebrew Christian community in 1884–85. Rabinowitz took the community of Hebrew Christian believers out of the boundaries of established churches and kept it within the realms of the synagogue. A similar success occurred under the leadership of Rabbi Isaac Lichtenstein in Tapio-Szele, Hungary. The first Hebrew Christian Church in Buenos Aires, Argentina, was established in 1936, and similar churches were formed in different European countries. These and similar stories led to the analysis of the question of whether the time had arrived to "rebuild David's tabernacle that is fallen down" by establishing independent Jewish congregations. This question led to the setting up of a committee to study the viability of Hebrew Christian churches. This landmark event took place at the Budapest Conference of the IHCA, the last conference before the Holocaust. By then, there were several Hebrew Christian churches in Europe and North and South America. But the tragedy of the Holocaust necessitated Jewish believers to shift gears from establishing indigenous congregations to escaping Hitler's camps and assisting refugees.

After Judaism was back on its feet again, the Jewish believers continued their spiritual quest. Thus, the Hebrew Christian movement began slowly to transform itself into Messianic Judaism as we know it today. In some places, it was a sharp breakaway from the gentile church, while in others, the process was much smoother. Out of the ashes of the Holocaust and with the founding of the modern State of Israel, a new Jewish identity began to develop and the Hebrew Christian movement was not immune to these changes. The term Hebrew Christian no longer properly defined Jewish believers in Yeshua, therefore a more adequate form of expressing their Jewish identity and belief was found in the term Messianic Jew.

Unity Within Diversity

Today there are as many forms of Messianic Judaism around the world as there are forms of Judaism. In most instances, Messianic Jewish congregations are molded after the milieu of which they are a part. In the United States, where the largest number of Messianic Jews reside, congregations tend to adopt more parts of the traditional Jewish synagogue service, with their own Siddur, Torah Scrolls, etc. On the other hand, in Great Britain, where the Hebrew Christian movement was stronger, Messianic Judaism was slow to adopt traditional Jewish elements. Argentina, with a European evangelical tradition, was slow to accept changes; but even though the largest number of Jewish believers are part of traditional evangelical churches, Messianic Jewish congregations are well established. In Holland, most Jewish believers adopted the New Testament name given to the early followers of Yeshua, "HaDerech," the Way.

One of the hardest issues that Messianic Judaism is confronted with is the rejection suffered from mainline Judaism that, for the most part, argues that Jews who believe in Jesus have given up their Jewishness. Therefore, one of the things that engages Messianic Judaism is the need to prove that, even though it accepts Yeshua as the Messiah, it does not reject Jewishness as a lifestyle, a people and a culture. In addition to this, in the State of Israel Messianic believers struggle to have the same full rights under the Law of Return as all other Jews. In Russia and the former Soviet republics, there is a true awakening to Judaism and Messianic Judaism. Under the Communist regime, Judaism was suppressed and millions of Jews were alienated from their Jewish heritage. Now, with a new openness, not only are Jewish people rediscovering their Jewish heritage, but hundreds of them have come to accept the fact that Yeshua is the promised Messiah. Presently, there are Messianic Jewish congregations formed in St. Petersburg, Moscow and Kiev, and the testimony is being carried to other former Soviet republics.

By the end of 1993, there were 165 independent Messianic Jewish congregations world-wide, and a similar number of Jewish ministries and fellowships. Most Messianic Jewish congregations are affiliated with larger associations. Among these associations are the Union of Messianic Jewish Congregations, the International Alliance of Messianic Congregations and Synagogues, the Fellowship of Messianic Jewish Congregations, the Canadian Fellowship of Messianic Congregations and Ministries, the Southern Baptist Messianic Fellowship, etc. In spite of the different backgrounds, the Messianic Jewish movement is quite cohesive. The fundamental fact is not what makes these groups different, rather, what is the bond that holds them together in spite of it all. This bond is the belief that Yeshua is the Jewish Messiah, and that this belief does not make them forfeit their Jewishness.

Building Bridges or Building Walls?

While many in Orthodox Judaism have put their hopes in a modern messiah, who has not acknowledged himself to be the Messiah and who poorly meets the biblical requirements, Messianic Jews believe that the promised Messiah already came, and he was Yeshua of Nazareth. For many in traditional Judaism, this belief automatically disenfranchises the Messianic Jews from Judaism. Messianic Judaism responds that Yeshua and Judaism are not irreconcilable, but that Yeshua is the Jewish Messiah according to the Jewish Scriptures. On the other hand, can traditional Christian churches accept Messianic Judaism as a genuine biblical movement? Many have argued that Messianic Judaism is trying to build back the "middle wall of partition" torn down by the Messiah. To them, Messianic Judaism replies that the early church was mainly Jewish, and that neither Yeshua nor the apostles renounced their Judaism. The New Covenant speaks of the Messianic faith being taken to non-Jewish nations. The early Jewish believers truly rejoiced that finally, through Yeshua, Israel had come to be a light to all the nations. But as more and more gentiles accepted the Jewish Messiah as their personal savior, gradually the Jewish roots were either forgotten or consciously removed. The fact is that for centuries, when a Jew believed in Yeshua, he had to become in practice and faith a gentile. Messianic Judaism tries to reverse this view and holds the right to believe in Yeshua within its own Jewish context.

Since, historically, the Church has failed to reach out to the Jewish people, Messianic Judaism can be the bridge to reach them. The Church should welcome this opportunity for Messianic Judaism to be God's appointed instrument for this historic time.

17

Messianic Believers in Israel and Their Messiah

Bodil F. Skjøtt

How many Jews in Israel believe that Jesus (or "Yeshua" in Hebrew) is the promised Messiah? Had this question been asked not today but 2000 years ago, the number would for sure have been in the thousands, according to the New Testament book of Acts. Hundreds of years later there were very few, if any, Jews in the Holy Land who confessed Jesus as their Messiah. Anyone reporting on the religious scene there would have justifiably not mentioned Jesus-believing Jews at all.

Today the situation is different. The number of Messianic Believers is not as high as 2000 years ago, but neither can they be ignored. In an accurate assessment of the religious scene in Israel today, mention of Jesus-believing Jews is essential. Information on the actual number varies. One source quotes their number in the hundreds while others inflate the number and quote it in the tens of thousands. The Messianic Believers themselves claim 2000–3000 adherents. Regardless, the number is minute. Their presence and contribution to everyday life in Israel can, however, no longer be ignored.

From Dan to Beersheba

Messianic congregations or groups of Believers can today be found in almost any part of the country. The largest group of congregations is in Jerusalem, but also in the Tel Aviv area one finds many congregations and groups. Presently the number of groups is close to 40. Some congregations are more established than others and have existed even as far back as the 1960's, whereas other groups were formed only within the last years. Some meet in private homes and others have managed to rent a small place for their regular meetings. Also the number in each group varies greatly. Some count the attendance in the sixties and seventies or even higher. Others are more correctly described as house-groups, made up of 15–20 people. The existence of these small groups can easily be influenced by two or three families moving to a new place. As families come and go, new fellowships form, especially in areas of the country further away from more permanent congregations.

It is difficult, if not impossible, to describe the Messianic congregations in a way that will include all of them. Any description will challenge the exception. What they have in common is their faith that Jesus of Nazareth is the Jewish Messiah and their claim that this faith does not make them non-Jews. Many will even say that only after coming to faith in Jesus of Nazareth as the Messiah did they discover their own Jewish identity in a meaningful way.

Some congregations have or had closer ties with a foreign organization, but they all believe very strongly in the self-rule of the local congregation. The leadership is handled by a group of leaders or elders, often with one person doing more of the work and being referred to as the pastor. No formal structure exists that ties the individual groups together in a recognized organization. But the different groups still relate to and cooperate with each other from time to time. This is true in the area of children's and youth work, in evangelistic efforts, and also when it comes to music and worship. Often congregations will come together to celebrate the holidays together.

For more than 10 years conferences for congregational leaders have been held on a national level. Even though not all groups are actively involved, this structure has proven helpful. It has served as a unifying factor, raising the profile of cooperation and the profile of the Jesus-believing Jews within Israeli society in general. The leaders' conference and other joint activities have caused the Believers to be more visible to the rest of society. These structures, even though rather loose, have conveyed the message to people outside that the Messianic Believers are not just a few individual people with a strange conviction but they are, in spite of their differences, a movement representing all streams of society.

Saturday — A Day of Rest — A Day of Worship

Most congregations meet for regular worship on Saturday, adapting themselves to the rhythm of the rest of society. It is the day of rest and the day in which most people are free to come. Some groups choose Saturday out of theological reasons. Others prefer not to travel on the Sabbath and meet only after sunset. Some groups find a regular weekday more convenient for them and prefer to keep Sabbath a family and rest day.

Their language and style of worship are adapted to Israel. For some, this means the order of worship is that of the service of the synagogue. The language used is Hebrew and translation into other languages is provided according to need. Whether the style of worship is inspired by the synagogue service or not, the aim is to create a form of worship with songs, prayer and teaching where Israelis feel at home. New music has been composed for Scripture passages, and songs have been written communicating faith in Yeshua in the language and the context of the Israeli society.

Just as it is natural for most Messianic Believers to come together for worship on the Sabbath because it is the day of rest, so they also keep the other Jewish holidays. Israel has both national and biblical holidays in which Messianic Jews take part. There are different opinions among them as to what part of the Jewish traditions to keep, but the majority of Messianic Believers observe the elements that are biblical and which remind them of the history of Israel and God's election, redemption and final hope for his people.

Messianic Believers celebrate *Pesach* (Passover) and remember how Israel was redeemed from slavery. But they will also remember that Jesus interpreted this in light of his own death and resurrection. Many Messianic congregations have written their own *Pesach Haggadah* (Passover liturgy). Other religious holidays are celebrated too, using the biblical traditions and remembering how Jesus himself celebrated these feasts, often relating them to his own life. Just as Jesus did not do away with the feasts and traditions of Israel, but observed them, Messianic Believers do the same, recognizing that Jesus completed and fulfilled God's salvation plan.

Evangelism

The group of Jewish people who 2000 years ago proclaimed Jesus of Nazareth to be the Messiah had a desire to share this conviction with the rest of Jewish society. Messianic Believers today also believe that salvation for Jews and non-Jews alike is found in the faith that the God of Israel raised Jesus from the dead as Israel's Messiah. They share with the first Believers the desire to communicate this to the rest of Jewish society. The differences between the congregations are reflected in the way they involve themselves in evangelism and share their faith, but all of them are convinced that Jews do not have a separate way to God. The new covenant in Jesus the Messiah is not only for non-Jews, nor does it replace the old — rather it fulfills and completes it.

Over the last 10–15 years there has been a great change in the way the congregations involve themselves in active evangelism. Previously, most Believers were intimidated and many had experienced opposition and harassment from other groups within society. Opposition still exists and the congregations relate to that differently. But many Believers have realized that their conduct and life-style matter little to those opposed to their faith. Therefore they might as well be open about their belief and actively share their faith. This changed attitude is found especially among younger Believers who grew up in Israel and therefore feel more secure about their identity both as Believers in Jesus and as Israelis. As a result of this change, campaigns involving street evangelism and handing out of tracts and other literature have been organized on a regular basis over the last 10 years. Contacts are made with non-Believers and followed up by the congregations involved in the campaign.

Only 15 years ago, most people would say that this kind of activity could not be done in Israel. The first campaigns were all done in the area of Tel Aviv and later in Haifa in the north. Even thinking about street evangelism in Jerusalem seemed absurd. But even here the mentality has changed and, though no big campaign has yet been held in Jerusalem, individual congregations are involved in outreach activities there. They are finding that Israelis today are more open to consider the question of who Jesus is. Some of them might be unaware that this consideration used to be off limits for a Jew. Others feel the spiritual vacuum of living in a secular society and are seeking alternative answers even in what was once unthinkable.

Messianic Believers in the Israeli Press

From time to time Messianic Jews are mentioned in the Israeli press. When their evangelistic activities and street campaigns have been mentioned recently it has not been so much to ridicule and to capitalize on the danger for the rest of society. Rather, the press has reported disturbances caused by members of the religious Orthodox community, who have tried to hinder Messianic Believers in the exercise of their democratic right to express their faith.

More often the press has focused on the question of whether

or not a Jew can believe in Jesus and remain a Jew. The conviction among many religious Jewish people in Israel today is that faith in Jesus, whose Jewishness nobody denies, makes a person non-Jewish. It is said that being a follower of Jesus and therefore a member of a fellowship where he is proclaimed Lord and Savior means that one has left the covenanted community of Abraham and stopped being a Jew. It makes no difference that one's mother is Jewish. Only in one sense can a Jew who believes Jesus to be the Messiah remain a Jew: if he or she repents and returns.

Some Messianic Believers immigrating to Israel have been denied the right to citizenship. Because the authorities consider them non-Jews they do not qualify under the Law of Return. When this issue has been dealt with by the press it has also raised the awareness of Messianic Believers in general. Some Believers have felt intimidated by this, but negative effects on the community are hard to prove. Some would even say the opposite. Most secular Israelis do not agree with the position taken by the authorities and have taken the side of the Messianic Believers — if not out of sympathy with them then as a reaction to the religious monopoly of the Orthodox community. A majority of the Israeli public recognizes and accepts Messianic Believers as long as they behave well, are good citizens and contribute to the life of the society, something, according to the opinion of many secular Jews, not all Orthodox Jews do.

The way Messianic Believers are perceived by the rest of society together with the denial of their right to citizenship upon return to Israel relates to the question of who is a Jew.

Who is a Jew?

There is a legal side to this question as we have seen and, unfortunately, the legal answer to it does not at present favor Messianic Believers. But there is also an internal side to the question, which touches on the relation between the Jewish tradition and Jewish identity. This is a much more basic aspect of the question, and one that not only the followers of Jesus need to consider. In one way, they have struggled with it and their answer lies in their understanding of who Jesus is. Through their faith in him as their Messiah, they have accepted what the God of Israel all the time had intended for the Jewish people. Their understanding of what it means to be Jewish challenges the rest of Israeli society, especially those who are open enough to admit they are uncertain about the answer.

18

Jesus, Israel's Messiah — A Messiah for Israel

Tuvya Zaretsky

Due to poor health in the last two years of his life, Rebbe Schneerson had been able to say little that would verify his possible messiahship. With his death, the messianic hopes of the Lubavitcher Hasidim came crashing to earth. Two days after his burial, Emily Torgan reported in *The Jerusalem Post* the turmoil surrounding the Lubavitcher community at the Habad movement's headquarters in Crown Heights, Brooklyn.

> "I'm still internalizing it," said Rabbi Sholom Levitin. "I'm coming to grips with the fact that now the rebbe is no longer here on a physical plane. But he's taught us for 44 years, and will continue to guide us."
>
> "Habad will continue to grow based on the ground work of the movement," said Efraim Klein outside the

complex. "This is just the beginning. Many want to perpetuate his memory. I don't know whether he is or is not the moshiach now. But the pain means different things to different people."

"A miracle didn't come when he died, but one still could," said another Lubavitcher.

In the case of Jesus, the grave marked the start of all the messianic excitement. It was all just beginning right after he died!

Scripture Fulfilled

It was his resurrection that verified Yeshua (Jesus) as Messiah. Shortly after he accomplished the work of atonement at the cross, Jesus actually wanted to talk about his messiahship with some of his followers (Luke 24:26–27, 44–48). He asked: "Was it not necessary for the Messiah to suffer these things and to enter into his glory?"

Since people don't ordinarily rise up from the grave, Jesus could speak to his original Jewish followers with some authority about the importance of what had happened.

These are my words which I spoke to you while I was still with you, that all things which are written about me in the Law of Moses and the Prophets and the Psalms must be fulfilled (Luke 24:44).

Luke continued to describe how Jesus opened the minds of his disciples to understand the Scriptures when he said:

Thus it is written, that the Messiah should suffer and rise again from the dead the third day; and that repentance for forgiveness of sins should be proclaimed in his name to all the nations, beginning from Jerusalem (Luke 24:45–47).

Whereas, the death of Rabbi Schneerson was viewed by many

of his followers as the end of one messianic hope, the death of Yeshua was the specific verification of *his* unique anointing as *the* Son of God (Romans 1:1–4). That truth was not lost on his disciples. With astounding confidence and exhilaration, the result of being empowered by God's Spirit, they boldly proclaimed Jesus as Messiah.

At *Shavuot* (Pentecost) in Jerusalem, Peter enthusiastically addressed a crowd of Jews and gentile proselytes. Speaking for the other disciples, he told the gathering about the resurrected one. In fact, he said that they (Jesus' followers) had been anointed by the Spirit of God to tell "all the house of Israel...for certain that God has made him both Lord and Messiah — this Jesus whom you crucified" (Acts 2:36).

When Rabbi Schneerson died, many of his followers were confused. Their great expectations were disappointed. Like today, there was confusion about Messiah among Jewish people in the Second Temple Period. Though biblically accurate, the picture of the death and resurrection of Jesus just didn't square with the popular messianic expectation of that day. However, Jesus had clearly instructed his followers about Messiah's mission from the Hebrew Bible.

Yeshua and Biblical Messianic Images

The Hebrew word, which in English is transliterated Messiah, was the defining term for one who would be uniquely *anointed* as God's servant. Imagine the surprise of Yeshua's friends at his hometown synagogue in Nazareth when he introduced the anointed one of God. The scroll of the prophet Isaiah was handed to him so he read from Isaiah 61:1: "The Spirit of the Lord is on me, because he has anointed me to preach good news to the poor" (Luke 4:18). To the wonderment of all, he added, "Today this Scripture has been fulfilled in your hearing."

On several occasions, he explained that specific messianic passages of Scripture were written about him. For example, it was popularly understood among Jewish people that God's messianic servant would be one like Moses (Deuteronomy 18:15, 18). Jesus didn't hesitate to appeal to Moses saying, "If you believed Moses, you would believe me; for he wrote of me" (John 5:46). Clearly, the Nazarene had come to be Israel's Messiah, according to none other than Moses himself.

The Servant of Isaiah 53:12, was understood to give his life as a substitutionary sacrifice for the sin of transgressors. This passage was deemed messianic in a Midrash on Exodus (*Exodus Rabbah* 15 and 19), as expressed by the Jewish scholar A. Edersheim in the last century. Yeshua identified himself as that specific anointed Servant when he said, "For I tell you, that this which is written must be fulfilled in me, '*and he was numbered with transgressors*'; for that which refers to me has its fulfillment" (Luke 22:37).

Jesus was able to clear up the confusion about his messiahship. Even so, he was in such contrast to the popular expectation that Jewish leaders reacted with incredulity. The religious Council, the Sanhedrin, convened as a Bet-Din to try him for blasphemy. Caiaphas, the high priest, demanded of Yeshua a defense of his messiahship. With lofty eschatological images from the book of Daniel, he exceeded their fears about him saying, "You have said it *yourself*, nevertheless I tell you, hereafter you shall see *the Son of Man sitting at the right hand of power, and coming on the clouds of heaven*" (Matthew 26:64).

Had Caiaphas and the elders judging Jesus seriously considered Yeshua's messiahship a possibility, they certainly would have treated him differently. So in response to their skepticism, he informed them that he was full of surprises, beyond their wildest messianic dreams. After all, he was Israel's Messiah!

Reluctance or Uncertainty

Still, Jesus was often reluctant to receive the public acclaim of messiahship. He occasionally had to confront and reject the contemporary Jewish yearning for a Messiah who would provide national liberation and autonomy from Rome (e.g., John 6:15). Was that unwillingness rooted in uncertainty, humility or sagacity?

For example, during the feast of *Hanukkah* (Feast of Dedication), in the city of Jerusalem, Jewish people were publicly asking him, "How long will you keep us in suspense? If you are the Messiah, tell us plainly" (John 10:24–25). He had confirmed that fact for them already. So, his reply illuminated the skepticism behind their question, "I told you, and you do not believe." At another time, the Sanhedrin received a similar answer for the same reason, "If I tell you, you will not believe" (Luke 22:67). Likewise, to his trusted Jewish followers, he confirmed as correct Simon Peter's declaration, "You are the Messiah" (Matthew 16:16). So, on occasion, he said plainly that he was at least *Messiah-elect.* Still, he asked the disciples to keep it quiet until his atoning work had been accomplished. Only then was all mystery removed. In his death, burial and resurrection Jesus was verified as Israel's Messiah.

Thus his reluctance to take up the honor and title of Messiah had little to do with uncertainty. Only after the proof in his resurrection does Jesus pull the picture together, "Was it not necessary for *the Messiah* to suffer these things and to enter into His glory?... And beginning with Moses and all the prophets, He explained to them the things *concerning Himself* in all the Scriptures" (Luke 24:26–27). Only after certainty is realized in his atonement and resurrection, does Yeshua finally seem to say, "This which has happened, is that which was foretold."

The non-Christian Jewish scholar, David Flusser, studied writings from the Qumran sect and Rabbi Akiva's letters found at Murabba'at, south of Qumran. Flusser's interpretation of the data from Jewish writings on the concept of Messiah yielded a helpful observation: "From the strictly theological point of view no man can be defined as a messiah before he has accomplished the task of the anointed." Thus, Yeshua's reluctance to claim the messianic title was appropriate. The contemporary Jewish view in his day held that the function and work of Messiah had to be completed first, before the title could be rightly claimed. He rightly was Israel's Messiah.

The Messiah for Israel — According to the Scriptures
Simon Peter was transformed by his personal encounter with

the resurrected Jesus. The Holy Spirit empowered Peter to give a speech at the Jaffo Gate of the Temple. His words declared how Jesus fulfilled the biblical expectation of Messiah.

> But the things which God announced beforehand by the mouth of all the prophets, that his Messiah should suffer, he has thus fulfilled. Repent, therefore, and return, that your sins may be wiped away, in order that times of refreshing may come from the presence of the Lord; and that he may send Jesus, the Messiah, appointed for you (Acts 3:18–20).

Jesus' followers were confident to declare Messiah to Jewish people in and outside of Israel. "And every day, in the Temple and from house to house, they kept right on teaching and preaching Jesus as Messiah" (Acts 5:42). In Samaria, Philip boldly preached (Acts 8:5) and outside of Israel, other followers spoke of Jesus the Messiah among the Jews of Damascus, Thessalonica and Corinth (Acts 9:22; 17:1–3; 18:5, 28). According to Richard Longenecker, "Basic to the christology of the earliest Jewish Christians was the conviction of Jesus as the Messiah."

Jesus — Still the Messiah for Israel

As shown previously, Jesus saw his ministry as fulfilling Scripture. He also initiated post-resurrection discussion about his messiahship as based in the Hebrew Bible. The Apostle Paul penned, "For whatever was written in earlier times was written for our instruction, that through perseverance and the encouragement of the Scriptures we might have hope" (Romans 15:4). The Alexandrian-born and eloquent Jewish Believer, Apollos, powerfully demonstrated "by the Scriptures that Jesus was the Messiah" (Acts 18:28). Because Jesus based his claim upon the Bible, he is *still* Israel's Messiah.

A Messiah who dies and who stays dead, is no anointed redeemer. By his resurrection, Messiah Yeshua was declared "the Son of God with power" (Romans 1:4). The heart of the good news is "that Messiah died for our sins according to the Scriptures...and that he was raised on the third day according to the Scriptures" (1 Corinthians 15:3–4, 20). Indeed, "Messiah has been raised from the dead, the first fruits of those who are asleep." Because Jesus was resurrected, he is *still* the Messiah for Israel.

The good news about Jesus is not merely a truth, as if one of many opinions. He is *the* truth. In his own words, he said, "I am the way, and the truth, and the life; no one comes to the Father, but through me" (John 14:6). Because Yeshua is true, he is *still* truly Messiah today.

A Personal Question

How will you respond to the truth that Yeshua is the Messiah for Israel today? John the Apostle was one early Jewish Christian who said that everything he wrote was "written that you may believe that Jesus is the Messiah, the Son of God; and that believing you may have life in his name" (John 20:31). You can ask God, right now, to enable you to believe and receive his Messiah.

19

My Way To The Messiah

Stan Telchin

My parents were like the couple in *Fiddler On The Roof.* They fled Russia in 1904 to get away from the pogroms and the antisemitism that was rampant there. My father, grandfather and uncles came to New York City with little more than the clothes on their backs. Even though they did not know English they were soon able to get jobs to support themselves. Two years later they had saved enough to bring my mother, grandmother and assorted aunts and cousins to the United States. Over the years that followed six children were born into our family. In 1924 I was born, the youngest member of the family.

"Them Christians"

I think that the first time I ever heard the word "Messiah" used was when I was about seven and we were in the midst of the depression. I asked my mother for something which we could definitely not afford. She laughingly told me that I could have it

"Ven de Meshiach kumt" (when the Messiah comes). I wasn't sure what that meant, but I knew that I would not be getting the thing I had asked for. The next time I heard the word Messiah was when the news of the Holocaust exploded in our midst. That is when I heard my mother praying and asking God to send the Messiah to deliver us from the hatred of the world.

Though my grandparents were ultra Orthodox, my parents were more conservative in their observance of Jewish customs and rituals. As I think back over the years of my growing up, I know that we often went to the synagogue, but I can't remember my parents ever really talking with me about God and we never talked about the Messiah.

I experienced a great deal of antisemitism when I was growing up. There was no getting away from the fact that there was "us Jews" and "them Christians." You see we thought that anyone who wasn't Jewish was automatically a Christian. I learned at a very early age that the further I stayed away from "them," the easier my life would be. And so I stayed away from "them" as much as I could.

I Felt Betrayed

With that as background, we can now go forward in time to September 1974 when we lived in Bethesda, Maryland. My wife, Ethel, arranged a huge party for my 50th birthday. Ethel is a wonderful woman and we have had an exceptionally happy marriage. We also have been blessed with two beautiful daughters, Judy and Ann. We had a very large home complete with swimming pool, four BMW's and full-time help. I was very successful financially. Then, just months later, my world seemed to be coming to an end. My daughter Judy who was a student at Boston University called me one Sunday evening. I knew that something was wrong from the very moment I picked up the phone. In a forty-five minute telephone conversation Judy explained that she had come to believe that Jesus is the Messiah! I was almost speechless. I was outraged. I felt betrayed. How could a child of mine join the enemy? As the conversation continued, I realized I had two options: I could disown her immediately for this terrible act or I could love her through it. I decided on the second option.

Two weeks later Judy came home for spring vacation. We talked and talked and talked. I don't remember much of what Judy said, but I remember that I kept saying "But Judy, you are Jewish! You *can't* believe in Jesus! You can't be Jewish and believe in Jesus!" to which she would reply, "Daddy, that isn't true. Jews have always believed in Jesus!" Just before she left to return to school, Judy challenged me to do something I had never done. "Daddy, you are an educated man. You have all kinds of degrees. Read the Bible for yourself and make up your own mind. It is either true or it is false. And if you read it carefully and ask God to reveal the truth to you, he will."

I Decided to Read the Bible

I understood what Judy wanted to accomplish by that challenge, but I saw it as a way to disprove what she believed. Immediately I decided to read the Bible and from it I planned to gather enough information to prove that Jesus is *not* the Messiah. By doing so, I would win her back!

After dinner the very next night I picked up the New Testament for the very first time. As I set out to read the book of Matthew, I was prepared for a book of hate aimed at the Jewish people. What else could it be? "The Christians get their hate for us either from their mother's milk or from this book," I thought. But I didn't find it to be a book of hate. It was a book written by a Jew, for other Jews, about the God of Abraham, Isaac and Jacob and the Messiah he sent to his people.

The next night I read the book of Mark. On Wednesday night I read Luke. On Thursday and Friday nights I read John. My note pad was filling up with lots and lots of questions. On Saturday morning I began to read The Acts of the Apostles. All went well until I came to the 10th chapter of this book. There I read about Peter reluctantly going to the house of Cornelius, a Roman centurion — a gentile. Peter didn't want to be there. He didn't want to be with this gentile. But Cornelius explained that he had had a vision and that in that vision he was told that Peter would tell him about God. With that prompting, Peter began to tell Cornelius about the God of Abraham, Isaac and Jacob and about Jesus, the Messiah. While he was speaking something totally unexpected happened: the Holy Spirit fell upon Cornelius and on all the gentiles in his home. Peter and the Jewish believers who were with him were astonished. How could this be. How could the Holy Spirit fall upon these gentiles? That wasn't supposed to happen! The Holy Spirit of God had been given to the Jews! He hadn't come to the gentiles!

In the next chapter of Acts, I read about how Peter was in Jerusalem at a meeting of the Jerusalem Council. The Jewish believers at that meeting were very upset with Peter because he had eaten with a gentile and shared the Messiah with him. But Peter explained what had happened and how the Holy Spirit had fallen on the gentiles in Cornelius' house. At this report, the Council decided that God is not a respecter of persons and that the Messiah must be for the gentiles as well as the Jews! As I read these things, I was stunned. How could this be? How was it possible that 2000 years ago the Messiah was only for Jews and not for the gentiles — and now he is only for the gentiles and not for us? What happened over the years?

Do I Really Believe in God?

As I set out to study the matter, I remember writing down a series of significant questions. Each question led to the next. "Do I really believe in God?" "Do I believe that the Tanakh, the Jewish Scriptures, is God's Word to us or is it only the story of the Jewish people?" "Does the Tanakh prophesy about a Messiah who is to come?" "Has anyone ever lived who fulfilled these prophecies?" "Did Jesus fulfill them?" I knew that if I received a "no" answer to any of these questions, my study would be over. But if each question produced a "yes" answer I was in serious trouble because the last thing in the world that I wanted to believe was that Jesus is the Messiah.

The next days, weeks and months were filled with study for

me. After a few days, I took a leave of absence from my business so that I could have more time to study. I read the entire New Covenant, or the New Testament, and a good portion of the Tanakh. I went to the library and obtained books about the Jewish religion and Jewish history. I talked to rabbis. I studied the prophecies in the Tanakh. I don't know how many prophecies it contains about the Messiah, but I came up with a list of over 40 of them. And it staggered me to realize that Jesus fulfilled each of them! Of particular significance to me in my study was Jeremiah 31 where God promised a New Covenant to the Jewish people! How could I have been 50 years old and not known of this promise? And then there was Proverbs 30 which spoke of God's Son, and Psalm 22 which revealed Jesus hanging on that tree, and Isaiah 53 which explained that our sins were placed upon him and he was punished in our stead, and Daniel 9 which prophesied that Jerusalem and the Temple would be destroyed by the prince who would come, after the Messiah had been cut off! I knew when these things took place. They happened in the year 70CE! I was stunned by this realization. I remember writing, "Either the Messiah came and died before the year 70 or the Bible is merely the story of the Jewish people and not the word of God!" The more I thought about the Scriptures I studied, the more convinced I became that Jesus really is the Jewish Messiah. And that is something I did not want to believe!

But I decided to attend a meeting of "Messianic Jews," Jews who believe that Jesus is the Messiah. At this meeting I met a woman named Lillian. When she found out that I was not yet a believer in Jesus, she offered me her Bible and asked me to read Exodus 20:2–3 aloud to her. I opened the Bible and read: "I am the Lord thy God, which have brought thee out of the land of Egypt, out of the house of bondage. Thou shalt have no other gods before me." When I finished reading, Lillian asked me to close the Bible and then said: "Tell me Stan, who is your God? Is He the God of our Fathers, the God of Abraham, Isaac and Jacob or are you worshipping false Gods like your business, your home, your wife, your children? What do you spend your time thinking about? Who do you worship?" I was struck by Lillian's questions and realized that I spent my time thinking and even worshiping each of these other things, but I almost never thought about God or worshiped him. Lillian's questions did their work and the pressure within me kept building. I knew that in my heart I believed that Jesus is the Messiah, but I was afraid to confess this with my mouth. I was afraid of the consequences such a decision would have on my life, on the life of my family and on my business. I remember arguing with myself. I remember raising the objections of the Crusades and the Inquisition and the Pogroms and the Holocaust. As if to answer each argument I would raise, on the inside of me I would hear: "Yes, but it's true!"

The next day, 3 July 1975 at 7:15 in the morning, the pressure within finally found it's release. It burst forth from my lips. Jesus is our Messiah! He is my Messiah. And I received him as Lord of my life.

The Messiah's Way To Me

I have studied the Scriptures diligently in the years since then. And you must know that if I was convinced in 1975 that Jesus is who he declared himself to be, I am even more convinced today.

In Deuteronomy 4:29 we read "If thou shalt seek the Lord thy God, thou shalt find him, if thou seek Him with all thy heart and all thy soul." It was in the Scriptures that I sought the Messiah. And it was through the Scriptures that he revealed himself to me.

So you see, the title of this chapter shouldn't be "My Way To The Messiah." It really should be "The Messiah's Way To Me."

20

The Coming Messiah and the Return of Jesus

Kai Kjær-Hansen

In Jerusalem, in the autumn of 1992, there were banners put up by the Habad movement carrying the message: "Prepare for the coming of the Messiah." At the same time about 200 Messianic Jews participated in the so-called Jerusalem March, which attracts many groups, both Jewish and Christian, in connection with the celebration of the Feast of the Tabernacles. The message on their banners was: "We are waiting for the return of the Messiah."

The question is whether there is some kind of connection between the coming Messiah of the Jews and the returning Messiah Jesus — or even common identity?

Some people seem to think so.

Will the Coming Messiah Be Identical with Jesus?

Some years ago I attended a lecture which a rabbi gave to a group of Christian tourists visiting Israel. In his lecture the rabbi touched upon the differences between Judaism and Christianity and why Jews do not think that Jesus was the Messiah. He said something along these lines: "I have a feeling that when the Messiah comes, he will be recognized both by us Jews and you Christians — and you will see him as the returning Jesus."

I remember that there were some in this tourist group who accepted this idea enthusiastically. The problem is that such people jump to conclusions. Those who are willing to listen to the New Testament in this matter reach a different conclusion.

Past — Future — Present

The first people to accept Jesus as the Messiah were Jews. In the New Testament they testify to their faith in Jesus as Messiah. The main part of the 27 books of the New Testament are written by Jesus-believing Jews. They make no attempt to hide that from the beginning they had the greatest difficulty grasping that Jesus should be the suffering Messiah. But after his resurrection they understood his messiahship.

- Jesus the Messiah came in weakness. This is the past.
- Jesus the Messiah will come in power and glory. This is the future.

And while they let their lives be determined by this past and this future, they experience that the crucified and resurrected Jesus comes to them — in their present — when they gather in his name. He is a living reality.

When the first Jesus-believing Jews dealt with this theme, there was no wavering. The Messiah they were waiting for would be identical with Jesus of Nazareth, the Messiah. And the work which Jesus did in the past needed no repetition and no supplement.

The author of Hebrews makes this clear. Having spoken, in chapter 9, of the once-and-for-all quality of the redemptive death of Jesus he goes on:

> And just as it is appointed for men to die once, and after
> that comes judgment, so Christ, having been offered once

to bear the sins of many, will appear a second time, not to deal with sin but to save those who are eagerly waiting for him (Hebrews 9:27–28).

There are many details regarding the return of Jesus which, if known, would clarify some of the conflict between variant views. But for now, believers will just have to cooperate even though there is some confusion about the details of his return.

Three Important Points

Yet, in the light of the New Testament three points are clear:

- First, when Jesus comes again, he will not come to atone for sin by dying again. This has been done once and for all.
- Second, he will come to save those who are waiting for him and who have trusted in him. It is the same Jesus who was taken up into heaven who will come again. It is the crucified and risen Jesus whom the believers are expecting.
- Third, exactly because it is the return of Jesus that the believer is looking forward to, it is out of the question that one should look for a person on this earth who might seem suited to be Messiah — no matter what qualities such a person might possess.

Rightly understood, there is every reason to prepare for the coming of the Messiah — to use a slogan from the Habad movement. That means prepare to receive the salvation which Jesus has brought through his death, and welcome him when he comes again.

The death of Jesus the Messiah can only be understood rightly in the light of the resurrection of the same Jesus and the hope of the return of the same Messiah.

Faith in the crucified and risen Jesus gives hope to a death-cursed humanity.

This is an assertion of faith. It can be verified only by someone who is willing and courageous enough to get to know him of whom the first Jesus-believing Jews testify — Jesus the Messiah.

Glossary

Amidah, lit. "standing." A prayer to be recited while standing. It is part of the obligatory prayers known as the "Eighteen Benedictions."

Amora (pl. *Amoraim*). Designation of the scholars active from the period of the completion of the Mishnah (200AD) until the completion of the two Talmuds.

Bar Mitzvah, lit. "son of a commandment." When a boy reaches the age of 13 Jewish law recognizes his religious responsibility; a ceremony is held at which the boy is called up in the synagogue to read a portion of the Torah.

Bat Yam. City in Israel, just south of Tel Aviv.

Beraita (pl. *Beraitot*). Aramaic word meaning "outside teaching"; tannaitic teaching not included in the Mishnah, collected in the Tosefta or the halakhic Midrashim.

Bet-Din, lit. "house of judgment." A term used in rabbinic sources for a Jewish court of law.

Birkat ha-minim, lit. "benediction concerning heretics." The 12th benediction in the Amidah. In the version ascribed to Samuel the

Little (end of 1st century AD) the term *minim* refers to sectarians and heretics as seen by the Pharisees, including Jesus-believing Jews.

Gemara, lit. "completion." The discussion on the Mishnah; Gemara and Mishnah together make up the Talmud.

Habad, also spelled *Chabad.* An acronymic abbreviation of the Hebrew terms for the higher faculties of wisdom (*Chochmah*), understanding (*Binah*) and knowledge (*Daat*).

Haggadah, lit. "narration." The name given to the book containing the order of service for the *Pesach* (Passover) meal.

Halakhah. Legal part of rabbinic literature.

Hanukkah. The name of the Jewish feast celebrating the rededication of the Temple after the Maccabean Revolt in 168BC.

Hasid, (pl. *Hasidim*), lit. "pious." The name given to followers of the religious and mystical revival movement among Jews in Russia and Poland in the 18th century.

Kabbalah. Jewish mystical writing.

Kashrut, lit. "proper." A collective term for laws regulating Jewish diet.

Lubavitch. The Orthodox Jewish sect headquartered in Brooklyn, New York, led by Rabbi Schneerson from the early 1950's until his death in 1994.

Messiah, from the Hebrew word *mashiach*; lit. "anointed." Rendered *Moshiach* when influenced by Yiddish.

Midrash, (pl. *Midrashim*); lit. "inquiry." Rabbinical commentary on Scripture.

Min, (pl. *Minim*). Technical term for sectarians and heretics.

Mishnah, lit. "repetition." The Oral Law, representing the interpretation of the Bible and the accumulation of legal traditions, the first and most authoritative section of the Talmud; completed c. 200AD.

Mitzvah, (pl. *Mitzvot*); lit. "commandment." Religious injunction and obligation; a good deed.

New Covenant. A designation for the New Testament often used by Messianic believers.

Pesach, in English "Passover." One of the three Jewish pilgrim festivals, celebrating the Exodus from Egypt.

Rebbe, Yiddish. Honorific title which Hasidic Jews give to one of their dynastic leaders; the title is used in order to distinguish a Hasidic leader from the traditional *Rav*.

Sanhedrin. A Hebraized form of the Greek word *synedrion*, which means assembly. At the time of Jesus this was the high court of the Jewish people, composed of 70 elders and the high priest.

Shema, lit. "hear." The prayer/declaration of God's unity, recited twice daily in the Jewish liturgy beginning with the words, "Hear, O Israel: the Lord our God, the Lord is One" (Deuteronomy 6:4).

Siddur, lit. "ordering." The name given to the Jewish prayerbook.

Shavuot, lit. "weeks"; in English "Pentecost." One of the three Jewish pilgrim festivals. It is a harvest feast but it also commemorates the giving of the Torah on Mt. Sinai.

Succot, lit. "booths"; in English "Feast of Tabernacles." One of the three Jewish pilgrim festivals commemorating the wandering of the people of Israel in the wilderness, when they lived in booths.

Talmud, lit. "instruction." The code of Jewish law composed of the Mishnah and Gemara; the Jerusalem Talmud was completed at the end of the fourth century, the Babylonian Talmud at the end of the fifth century.

Tanakh, acronym for *Torah* (the five books of Moses), *Nevi'im* (the Prophets) and *Ketuvim* (the Writings); the Jewish Holy Scriptures. The designations Tanakh (or *Tenach*) or Jewish Scriptures are often used by Jews instead of "Old Testament."

Tanna, (pl. *tannaim*). Rabbinic teachers of the first and second centuries, mentioned in the Mishnah.

Targum, (pl. *targumim*); lit. "translation." Refers to the Aramaic translations of various parts of the Bible.

Tikkun, lit. "mending." The means of spiritual improvement.

Torah, lit. "instruction." The Hebrew name of the five books of Moses. It often refers to both the written and oral codes of the Jewish law; commonly used as a synonym for Tanakh.

Tosefta, lit. "additions." A supplement to the text of the Mishnah, often a variation.

Yalkut Shimoni, usually referred to as "the Yalkut" of Simeon of Frankfurt (13th or 14th century); the best known and most comprehensive midrashic anthology; covers the whole Bible.

Yeshua. The Hebrew name of Jesus of Nazareth; often used by Messianic believers instead of "Jesus" to stress his Jewishness.

Yom Kippur, lit. "Day of Atonement." The purpose of the day is "repentance" by recognizing and confessing one's sins. It is a day of fasting.

Selected Bibliography

The chapter references in parentheses refer to the chapters in this book.

Abramowitz, Yosef I. "What Happens If the Rebbe Dies?" *Moment*, April 1993: 30–39, 70–75. (Chs. 1 and 2)

Baigent, Michael & Richard Leigh. *The Dead Sea Scrolls Deception*. London: Jonathan Cape, 1991. (Ch. 4)

Baron, David. *The Servant of Jehovah*. Grand Rapids: Zondervan, 1922. (Ch. 9)

Betz, Otto & Rainer Riesner. *Jesus, Qumran and the Vatican*. London: SCM Press, 1994. (Ch. 4)

Boteach, Shmuel. *The Wolf Shall Lie With the Lamb*. Northvale: Jason Aronson, Inc., 1993. (Ch. 10)

Brod, Menachem M. *Yemot Hamashiach...* [The Age of the Messiah: Redemption and the Coming of the Messiah in Jewish Sources]. Kfar Habad: Lubavitch Institute, 1992 (in Hebrew). (Ch. 11)

Dan, Joseph. *The Teachings of Hasidism*. New York: Behrman House, Inc., 1983. (Ch. 10)

Edersheim, Alfred. *The Life and Times of Jesus the Messiah*, 1886. Grand Rapids: Eerdmans Publishing Co., reprint 1971. (Ch. 18)

Elior, Rachel. *The Paradoxical Ascent to God.* Trans. Jeffrey Green. New York: State University of New York, 1993. (Ch. 10)

Ezra, Ibn. *The Commentary of Ibn Ezra on Isaiah.* Trans. M. Friedlander. New York: Philip Feldheim, 1873. (Ch. 9)

Fitzmyer, Joseph A. "Crucifixion in Ancient Palestine, Qumran Literature, and the New Testament," *Catholic Biblical Quarterly* 40, 1978. (Ch. 5)

Flannery, Edward H. *The Anguish of the Jews: Twenty-three Centuries of Antisemitism.* New York/Mahwah: Paulist Press, 1985. (Ch. 9)

Fruchtenbaum, Arnold. *Jesus Was a Jew.* San Antonio, Texas: Ariel Ministries, 1981. (Chapter 13 is adapted from this book with the permission of the author.)

Gaster, Theodore. *Festivals of the Jewish Year.* New York: Morrow Quill, 1978. (Ch. 7)

Greenstone, Julius. *The Messiah Idea in Jewish History.* Westport, Connecticut: Greenwood Press, reprint 1972. (Ch. 9)

Hengel, Martin. *Crucifixion in the Ancient World and the Folly of the Message of the Cross.* London: SCM Press, 1977. (Ch. 5)

Hertzberg, Arthur. "Waiting for the Messiah." *Commonwealth*, 8 May 1992: 11–13. (Ch. 10)

Hoffmann, Edward. *Despite All Odds: The Story of Lubavitch.* New York: Simon & Schuster, 1991. (Ch. 1)

Horowitz, Craig. "Holy War." *New York Magazine*, 14 February 1994: 27–34. (Ch. 10)

Josephus, Flavius. *Antiquities of the Jews.* Grand Rapids: Kregel Publications, 1960. (Ch. 7)

Kac, Arthur W. *The Messianic Hope.* Grand Rapids: Baker Book House, 1975. (Ch. 18)

Kjær-Hansen, Kai. *Joseph Rabinowitz and the Messianic Movement.* Edinburgh & Grand Rapids: The Handsel Press & Eerdmans Publishing Co., 1994. (Ch. 16)

Klausner, Joseph. *The Messianic Idea in Israel.* New York: The Macmillan Company, 1955. (Ch. 11)

Lagnado, Lucette. "Messiah Wars." *Voice*, 6 July 1993: 23–38. (Ch. 10)

Levine, Samuel. *You Take Jesus, I'll Take God.* Los Angeles: Hamoroh Press, 1980. (Ch. 15)

Levinson, Frederick. *Christian and Jew: The Life of Leon Levinson 1881–1936.* Edinburgh: The Pentland Press Ltd., 1989. (Ch. 16)

Longenecker, Richard N. *The Christology of Early Jewish Chistianity.* Grand Rapids: Baker Book House, 1970. (Ch. 18)

Maman Pinchas (ed.). *Torato shel Mashiach...*[The Teaching of the Messiah...]. Brooklyn, New York: Empire Press, 1993 (in Hebrew). (Ch. 11)

Moore, George F. *Judaism in the First Centuries of the Christian Era.* Vol. II. Cambridge, Massachusetts: Harvard University Press, 1927. (Ch. 9)

Patai, Raphael. *The Messiah Texts.* New York: Avon, 1979. (Ch. 9)

Pritz, Ray. *Nazarene Jewish Christianity: From the End of the New Testament Period Until Its Disappearance in the Fourth Century.* Jerusalem & Leiden: The Magnes Press & Brill, 1988. (Ch. 8)

Riggans, Walter. *Jesus Ben Joseph: An Introduction to Jesus the Jew.* Tunbridge Wells, England: Monarch Publication, Marc and Olive Press, 1993. (Chapter 14 is adapted from this book with the permission of the author.)

Rosen, Moishe. *Y'shua.* Chicago: Moody Press, 1982. (Ch. 18).

Rubin, Barry. *Facts About Firstfruits.* Baltimore: Lederer Publications, 1990, revised 1994. (Chapter 7 is adapted from this paper, with permission of the publisher.)

Scholem, Gershom. *The Messianic Idea in Judaism.* New York: Schocken Books, 1971. (Chs. 1 and 10)

Schonfield, Hugh J. *The History of Jewish Christianity: From the First to the Twentieth Century.* London: Druckworth, 1936. (Ch. 16)

Shamash, Jack. "Zealots for the Television Age." *New Statesman Society,* 15 May 1992: 20–21. (Ch. 10)

Shanks, Hershel (ed.). *Understanding The Dead Sea Scrolls.* New York: Random House, 1992. (Ch. 4)

Sibley, James R. "Trends in Jewish Evangelism." *Mishkan* 10, 1989: 24–38 (Ch. 17)

Silver, Abba Hillel. *A History of Messianic Speculation in Israel: From the First through the Seventeenth Centuries,* 1927. Boston: Beacon Press, reprint 1959; Gloucester, Massachusetts: Peter Smith, reprint, 1978. (Chs. 9, 11 and 12)

Stauffer, E. *Jerusalem und Rom im Zeitalter Jesu Christi.* Bern: 1957. (Ch. 5)

Stegemann, Hartmut. *Die Essener, Qumran, Johannes der Täufer und Jesus.* Freiburg/Basel/Wien: Herder, 1993. (Ch. 4)

Telchin, Stan. *Betrayed.* Old Tappan, New Jersey: Chosen Books, 1981. (Ch. 19)

Thiering, Barbara. *Jesus & the Riddle of the Dead Sea Scrolls: Unlocking the Secrets of His Life Story.* San Francisco: Harper, 1992. (Ch. 4)

Wolpo, Shalom Dov. *Yechi Hamelech Hamashiach.* [Long Live King Messiah]. Kiryat Gat, Israel: 1992 (in Hebrew). (Ch. 11)

Yadin, Yigael. *The Temple Scroll.* Vols. I–III. Jerusalem: The Israel Exploration Society, Hebrew edition 1977, English edition 1983. (Ch. 5)

Yadin, Yigael. "Pesher Nahum Reconsidered," *Israel Exploration Journal* 21, 1971: 1–12. (Ch. 5)

Author Information

OLE ANDERSEN is working with the Danish organization The Bible and Israel. He is Editor of the magazine *TEL*, published by the Danish Society of Biblical Archaeology. He holds an M.A. of Divinity from the University of Copenhagen.

CAROL CALISE is presently serving as Assistant Pastor at Beth Emanuel in Holbrook, New York. She is currently working on her Ph.D. in the Hebrew and Judaic Studies Department at the New York University.

TORLEIF ELGVIN is past Director of the Caspari Center for Biblical and Jewish Studies in Jerusalem. Presently he is Research Fellow at the Norwegian Lutheran School of Theology, Oslo and a member of the international team responsible for publishing the Dead Sea Scrolls.

ARNOLD FRUCHTENBAUM is Director of Ariel Ministries, Tustin, California. He holds a Th.M. from Dallas Theological Seminary and did his Ph.D. studies at New York University on Israelology.

ARTHUR F. GLASSER is Dean emeritus and Faculty coordinator of Judaic Studies and Jewish Evangelism at School of World Mission, the Fuller Theological Seminary, Pasadena, California.

LOUIS GOLDBERG is Professor of Theology and Jewish Studies at the Moody Bible Institute, Chicago. He is the author of biblical commentaries and books on Judaism and Messianic Jews.

NOAM HENDREN is a graduate of Dallas Theological Seminary in Dallas, Texas. He lives in Israel and is Pastor of the Messianic congregation Keren Yeshua in Kfar Saba, Israel.

KAI KJÆR-HANSEN has his Ph.D. on Studies in the Name of Jesus. He is presently working with the Danish Israel Mission and serves as the International Coordinator of the Lausanne Consultation on Jewish Evangelism (LCJE).

SAM NADLER is a Jewish believer and serves as President of Chosen People Ministries in Charlotte, North Carolina.

SUSAN PERLMAN is Assistant Executive Director of Jews for Jesus and Editor of the journal *Issues*. She is a member of the International Coordinating Committee of the Lausanne Consultation on Jewish Evangelism.

RAY PRITZ has his Ph.D. on Nazarene Jewish Christianity from the Hebrew University, Jerusalem. Presently he serves as the Coordinator of Hebrew language programs at the Caspari Center for Jewish and Biblical Studies in Jerusalem.

WALTER RIGGANS wrote his Ph.D. thesis on the Christology of the modern Messianic Jewish movement. He has been a Lecturer in Biblical and Jewish Studies. He is the General Secretary of Church's Ministry among the Jews, England (CMJ).

BARRY RUBIN is Executive Director of Lederer Messianic Ministries, Baltimore, Maryland. He is also the leader of Emmanuel Messianic Congregation, Columbia, Maryland.

TSVI SADAN holds an M.A. from Trinity Evangelical Divinity School in Chicago, Illinois. He is currently working with Netivyah Bible Instruction Ministry and is involved in establishing a Messianic college in Israel.

DAVID SEDACA is Secretary for the Americas of the International Messianic Jewish (Hebrew Christian) Alliance. He has served as lecturer and professor of Judaism in several seminaries in the United States and elsewhere.

BODIL F. SKJØTT is presently working with the Caspari Center for Biblical and Jewish Studies in Jerusalem. She serves as Editorial Secretary for the journal *Mishkan* and holds an M.A. of Divinity from the University of Aarhus, Denmark.

STAN TELCHIN has served for 14 years as Pastor of the Living Word Fellowship. He is the author of the book *Betrayed.* In 1994 he retired in order to write, travel and teach.

TUVYA ZARETSKY has served as Associate Executive Director of Jews for Jesus. Presently he is the Branch Leader of Jews for Jesus in Los Angeles. He is responsible for the "Israel Portfolio of Jews for Jesus".